MBAA Practical Handbook for the Specialty Brewer

Volume 3

Brewing Engineering and Plant Operations

Edited by Karl Ockert

BridgePort Brewing Company
Portland, Oregon

Master Brewers Association of the Americas

Cover photographs of brewery equipment courtesy of
BridgePort Brewing Company and (lower right) World Water Works

Library of Congress Control Number: 2005931016
International Standard Book Numbers:
0-9770519-1-9 (v. 1)   *Raw Materials and Brewhouse Operations*
0-9770519-2-7 (v. 2)   *Fermentation, Cellaring, and Packaging Operations*
0-9770519-3-5 (v. 3)   *Brewing Engineering and Plant Operations*

The Master Brewers Association of the Americas
3340 Pilot Knob Road
St. Paul, Minnesota 55121, U.S.A.

Contents

CHAPTER 5

Jim Kelter
Quality Assurance Brewmaster, Full Sail Brewing Company

Foreword

In 1944, four master brewers—Edward Vogel (Griesedieck Bros. Brewery, St. Louis, Missouri), Frank Schwaiger and Henry Leonhardt (Anheuser-Busch, St. Louis, Missouri), and J. Adolf Merten (Ems Brewing Company, East St. Louis, Illinois)—volunteered to write a manual for the brewery worker if the Master Brewers Association of the Americas would publish it. Two years later their labors produced *The Practical Brewer,* a work so fundamentally complete that it still has relevance sixty years later.

At a meeting of the Executive Committee of the Master Brewers Association of the Americas in January 2003 it was suggested that a new adaptation of *The Practical Brewer* be written in the original question-and-answer format. This endeavor would help the Association meet one of its purposes, to improve the art and science of brewing by disseminating information of value to its members, the profession, the brewing and associated industries, and the public.

The finished product should be useful for today's entire community of brewers, whether they work for craft or microbrewers or for large brewing companies or whether they are home brewers—all are certainly interested in expanding their knowledge of the art and science of brewing.

Jaime Jurado, of the Gambrinus Company, San Antonio, Texas, took up this suggestion and convinced Karl Ockert, of the BridgePort Brewing Company, Portland, Oregon, to be the editor-in-chief of the book. Karl recruited an excellent group of authors willing to volunteer their time and share their knowledge of brewing fundamentals with their brewing colleagues.

After much diligent work by everyone involved in this project, each chapter of this exciting new book, the *MBAA Practical Handbook for the Specialty Brewer,* has been written, edited, and reviewed and is ready to stand alongside *The Practical Brewer* as an exceptional resource of practical brewing fundamentals.

Like the authors of *The Practical Brewer*, published in 1946, the authors of the *MBAA Practical Handbook for the Specialty Brewer* are volunteers, who will receive no other reward than the thanks and appreciation of the Master Brewers Association of the Americas and the satisfaction of the completion of a job well done.

Frank J. Kirner

President, 2003
Master Brewers Association
of the Americas

Preface

The following pages were written by our colleagues in the spirit of camaraderie that sets the brewing industry apart from almost any other field. The authors wrote these chapters while continuing to meet the obligations of their busy professional schedules and their personal lives. None will collect a royalty or any other monetary payment for their efforts. They are all true professionals, and we benefit from the discussions they bring forth. That, to me, is what the MBAA is all about.

Each chapter is a distillation of the brewing knowledge that each writer possesses. The following chapters encompass not only the art and science of brewing as dogma but the education and experience that these writers have been exposed to during their careers.

It has been my honor and privilege to be a part of this project and to help the MBAA assemble this team of authors and then assist them in putting their works together for others to enjoy. In addition to the authors, I have had the pleasure of working with Frank Kirner, Inge Russell, Ray Klimovitz, Laura Harter, Gil Sanchez, Prof. Charlie Bamforth, Prof. Ludwig Narziss, and my friend and mentor, Prof. Emeritus Michael Lewis, all of whom have helped me with the challenging process of editing and refining this handbook.

I would like to thank the MBAA Districts Northwest, Texas, Eastern Canada, and New York, which helped sponsor the production of this book through their district treasuries.

Finally, I would especially like to thank Carlos Alvarez for allowing me to work on this book project and my wife, Carole Ockert, who allowed this project to take time away from our home life.

Karl Ockert
Editor-in-Chief
July 2005

Authors

Jaime Jurado is the director of brewing operations for the Gambrinus Company, in San Antonio, Texas. He holds undergraduate and graduate degrees in chemical and electrical engineering and has done postgraduate work in medical engineering. He was educated in brewing as a Praktikant in the Bavarian breweries of Patrizier-Brau AG, under the guidance of Dr. Ing. Peter Hellich and Dr. U. Ost, and has been in the professional brewing industry since 1983. He is active in the Draft Brewers Guild. Draft dispense application is his area of practical research.

Jim Kelter is the quality assurance brewmaster for the Full Sail Brewing Company, in Hood River, Oregon. He has worked for Full Sail since 1990. In addition to managing the quality assurance lab, he oversees brewing and packaging production and maintenance operations. He has been an active member of the company's safety committee. Full Sail recently received its fourth commendation from the Safety and Health Achievement Recognition Program of the Oregon Occupational Safety and Health Division, and the company is now working on its fifth.

Ashton Lewis is the master brewer at the Springfield Brewing Company, in Springfield, Missouri, and serves as an in-house brewing and food processing expert for SBC's parent company, Paul Mueller Company. Prior to joining Mueller in 1997, he taught brewing classes in the University of California extension program in Davis with Dr. Michael Lewis and Dr. Tom Shellhammer and was a partner in Lewis Twice and Shellhammer, a brewing consulting business. He earned a B.S. in food science and technology at Virginia Tech in 1991 and an M.S. in brewing science at the University of California, Davis, in 1994. As a graduate student, he worked at Sudwerk Privatbrauerei Hübsch, which then had many open fermenters, requiring manual cleaning. This task allowed plenty of time for pondering the subject of brewery sanitation! He is a member of the Master Brewers Association of the Americas and the Institute of Brewing and Distilling.

John Mallett is the production manager at the Kalamazoo Brewing Company, in Kalamazoo, Michigan. He has served in numerous capacities over his brewing career, as head brewer of the Commonwealth Brewery, in Boston, brewmaster at the Old Dominion Brewing Company, in Ashburn, Virginia, and founder and president of SAAZ, an equipment and service provider for breweries both large and small. He has lectured and written extensively, serves on various technical committees, and is widely known as a consulting resource. He attended the Siebel Institute and has been as a member of the extended faculty there.

Karl Ockert is the brewmaster and plant manager of the BridgePort Brewing Company, in Portland, Oregon, which he helped found and build in 1984. He earned a B.S. in fermentation sciences from the University of California, Davis, in 1983. His brewing career has covered the spectrum of breweries, ranging from brew pub size to the Anheuser-Busch brewery in Newark, New Jersey. His experience in environmental engineering comes from working with brewery plant wastewater disposal at BridgePort for the last nine years.

Fred Porter is the environmental engineer at the New Belgium Brewing Company, in Ft. Collins, Colorado. He earned a B.S. in chemical engineering from Colorado State University in 1997 and started work at New Belgium as a mechanic. He became facilities manager in 1998 and plant environmental engineer in 2003. His position at the brewery is devoted to managing an aerobic-anaerobic treatment plant installed in 2001.

CHAPTER 1

Plant Engineering, Utilities, and Process Control Equipment

John Mallett
Kalamazoo Brewing Company

1. What roles do the departments of engineering and maintenance perform?

Brewery workers are both enabled and limited by the equipment available for use. Engineering and maintenance are the disciplines that deal directly with these capabilities. Equipment that is malfunctioning, ill-maintained, or inappropriately selected presents real challenges to even very qualified brewery production personnel. Too often, expedient choices in equipment selection or maintenance reveal their true costs in compromised product, high labor costs from equipment downtime, or even objective safety hazards.

The engineering department works to find the best solutions within the constraints of space, time, budget, and flexibility, while the maintenance department assures the continued safe and proper operation of existing equipment. Breweries may have engineering and maintenance departments dedicated to the equipment that they are ultimately dependent on, or (especially in smaller plants) these responsibilities may fall under the purview of operators as ancillary duties. Installation of new equipment may be handled by either department or performed by an outside contractor. Knowledge and skills of particular relevance to these brewery disciplines include an understanding of plant equipment such as pumps and cooling systems, good mechanical skills, and familiarity with common brewery construction techniques and materials. An appreciation for brewery controls and electrical systems is increasing in importance.

The purpose of this chapter is to give the reader a rudimentary understanding of the vocabulary and concepts useful in these areas. Many of the calculations are greatly simplified; this is done purposely, to allow the reader to successfully perform "quick and dirty" calculations resulting in answers that provide rough orders of magnitude. A greater level of detail for most calculations may be found in the recognized brewing and engineering literature.

Materials

2. What materials are commonly used in brewery equipment?

Breweries are specialized sanitary food production facilities that utilize a variety of durable, yet easy-to-clean materials.

a. Copper was traditionally used for brewhouse vessels, because it is easy to work with and has superior heat-transfer properties. Cleaning copper is problematic, because it tends to degrade when common brewery cleaning agents are used. It has largely been supplanted by more modern materials.

b. Stainless steel is an alloy of iron, chromium, nickel, and in some cases molybdenum. The advantage of such an alloy is that it resists oxidative attack (rust) very well. The two main metallurgical series in brewery use are types 304 and 316. Brewhouse vessels, fermenters, and piping are commonly constructed of type 304. Type 316 is more resistant to corrosion and easier to machine but is more expensive. It is generally used for specialized fittings such as valves and pump parts. Stainless steel nuts, bolts, and common household pots generally are made of the less expensive 18-8 series alloys. Brewery equipment is fabricated mainly by the tungsten inert gas (TIG) welding process. The hot welding area is bathed in an argon blanket, which excludes oxygen and produces an exceptionally smooth and clean fusion area.

The most common surface finishes in the brewery are 2B, #4, and Brewery Quality (BQ). Finish 2B has a dull yet very smooth finish originating at the rolling mill. Finish #4 has a higher luster but is less smooth; it is a more expensive finish, achieved by surface grinding to 120–150 grit. It is used mainly for vessel exteriors where appearance is important. BQ is a finish used for pipes and fittings in large breweries. These finishes can be described by a roughness average (Ra) value, which relates to finish profile measured in microinches (millionths of an inch, or μin.). Electropolished goods have an Ra value of less than 10. Finish 2B has an Ra value between 20 and 60; a range of 30–70 is acceptable for #4; and that of the ID surface of BQ materials must be below 100.

Stainless steel for brewery use should be pickled or passivated. This process removes iron contamination, oxide scale, and other foreign material that may affect the appearance and/or corrosion resistance of the alloy. Stainless steel can be passivated by using a nitric acid blend or the safer and more environmentally benign citric acid (see Chapter 2, Volume 3, for a discussion of passivation).

Although stainless steel is able to resist oxidative attack well, it is not impervious. Chloride is particularly aggressive toward stainless steel. High concentrations of chloride, improper insulation material, heat, and crevices can singularly or jointly quickly destroy costly brewery equipment.

    c. Piping materials vary with application but may include

> Stainless steel, generally used for product transfer and also used for CO_2 supply to facilitate clean-in-place (CIP) operations
> Copper tube, used for water service and often for CO_2 and glycol piping
> Threaded steel pipe, used for both steam and natural gas supply; galvanized pipe is often used for compressed air
> PVC (polyvinyl chloride), used for drains, vents, glycol piping, and some water systems; threaded PVC fittings in glycol systems can be problematic because of cracking and failing

    d. Piping and tubing are sized by both their diameter and wall thickness.

Pipe is rated by a schedule that relates to wall thickness. Common schedules include 5, 10, 40, and 80. Pipe sidewall thickness increases with larger schedule numbers.

Copper tubing is of type K, L, or M. Type K is preferred for refrigeration applications, because it has the greatest sidewall thickness and is the most flexible. Type M is the least expensive, because of its thin sidewall, and is used mainly for residential applications. Type L is specified for most brewery applications. Copper may be silver-soldered for refrigeration or gas applications, but lead-free solder must be used for potable water service.

The seamless type 304 stainless tubing used for most wort and beer transfers is measured by its outside diameter. It has a wall thickness of

0.065 inch and is polished both internally and externally. Large breweries may use the less highly polished BQ schedule 5 stainless steel pipe for product transfer.

e. Insulation both saves energy and protects personnel from contacting equipment at dangerous temperatures. For materials that are warmer than ambient temperature, such as steam lines, fiberglass or the more ridged foam glass is commonly used. On heated brewery vessels, insulation with a very low chloride content, such as Inswool, should be used to prevent conditions under which a degradation of stainless steel called stress corrosion cracking (SCC) occurs. For applications colder than ambient temperature, care should be taken to select insulations with low water permeability. In these cold applications, condensation tends to inundate the insulation, if given the opportunity. For this reason, expanded polyethylene or polystyrene materials perform better than fiberglass or Armaflex materials. Regardless of the type of insulation, the exterior should be covered with a plastic or metal sheathing to protect it from physical damage and/or moisture uptake. Piping and insulation should always be labeled as to content and direction of flow.

f. Supports, piping, and other equipment are often supported with Unistrut, a preformed metal channel, and Allthread, a threaded rod. These supports are also available in stainless steel, which should be specified for use in wet areas. The amount of support required per linear foot of pipe run is specified for different types of piping and conduits. Commonly, racks are built and hung from the ceiling to support several types of utility piping as well as electrical conduits.

g. Electrical fittings in breweries are manufactured in a number of construction materials. Wiring conduits may be made of the watertight and flexible Sealtight-type, plastic, ridged aluminum, or the non-watertight EMT (electrical metallic tubing), depending on the application. Flexible electrical cord is generally of the SO family, such as SJOW (oil, weather, water, and sunlight resistant). In process areas, brewers should specify electrical installations adhering to the National Electrical Manufacturers Association (NEMA) 4 standard, which is defined as "protection against hose-directed water."

h. Quarry tile, epoxy grout, and fiberglass-reinforced plastic (FRP) panels are common industrial floor and wall coverings well suited to use in the brewery.

i. Elastomers are a class of compounds that act as sealing surfaces in brewery equipment. Common elastomers include Buna, EPDM, Neoprene, Silicone, Teflon, and Viton. These materials can be found in use as valve seats (internal seals), manway gaskets, pump seals, interfitting gaskets, and hose linings. The properties of each differ in flexibility, wear resistance, heat suitability, chemical compatibility, and cost. For example, Teflon is smooth, comparatively hard, and very inflexible. These properties make it well suited for rotating fittings but unacceptable for compression sealing duties. See question below dealing with various elastomers and their properties.

j. Ultra-high-molecular-weight (UHMW) plastic is well suited for low-friction duty, such as wear strips and handling parts on bottling lines.

k. Lubricants used in the brewery include various types of greases and machine lubrication oils. The ubiquitous WD-40 is an acid-based product best suited for freeing frozen or rusty assemblies. It is better to use light machine oils, such as 3 in 1 brand oil, for light lubrication. Food-grade lubricants are required wherever there is a possibility of product contamination.

l. Antiseize should be used on threaded stainless fittings because they are particularly susceptible to galling and seizing. It is recommended that this product be a nickel-based food-grade type. Vibrating hardware that is prone to loosening over time may benefit from a thread-locking compound.

3. What are the properties of some types of elastomers?

a. BUNA-N, nitrile, NBR

Temperature: –40° to 225°F (–40 to 107°C)
Pressure: max. 150 psi
Good resistance to oil and solvents
Moderate resistance to aromatics
Handles most food, dairy, beverage, and sanitary services
Excellent resistance to compression set, tear, and abrasion
Good resistance to acids and alkalis

b. Ethylene propylene diene terpolymer (EPDM)

Temperature: –65 to 350°F (–54 to 177°C); withstands short
    exposure to 400°F (204°C)
Pressure: max. 150 psi
Exceptional resistance to aging and high temperatures, moderate
    caustics, and acids

Excellent for hot water and steam service up to 325°F (163°C)

Very resistant to abrasion

Excellent resistance to ozone, sunlight, or weather and deionized water

Good tensile strength

Good resistance to mild acids, alkalis, and alcohols

c. Neoprene, chloroprene, polychloroprene, CR

Temperature: –20 to 180°F (–29 to 82°C)

Pressure: max. 150 psi

Originally developed as an oil-resistant substitute for natural rubber

Good resistance to solvents, acids, and abrasion

High resilience

Resists degradation from sun, ozone, and weather

Performs well in contact with oils and many chemicals

Remains useful over a wide temperature range

Displays outstanding physical toughness

Resists burning inherently better than exclusively hydrocarbon rubbers

Outstanding resistance to damage caused by flexing and twisting

d. Silicone

Temperature: –80° to 400°F (–62 to 204°C); withstands short exposure to 600°F (316°C)

Pressure: max. 150 psi

Excellent low-temperature flexibility

Good tolerance to high temperatures

Not resistant to abrasions and cuts

Poor resistance to alkalis and acids

Withstands many chemicals and combinations of chemicals

High standard of purity and non-leaching characteristics

Popular with the pharmaceutical industry

e. Teflon, polytetrafluoroethylene (PTFE), AFMU

Temperature: –40 to 500°F (–40 to 260°C)

Pressure: max 300 psi

Excellent resistance to high temperatures and chemicals

Poor ability to create a seal

Excellent performance properties
Excellent resistance to weather, heat, steam, abrasion, acid, petroleum oil, and vegetable oil

Teflon is a registered trademark of DuPont.

f. Viton, fluorocarbon rubber, hexafluoropropylene–vinylidene fluoride copolymer

Temperature: –20 to 400°F (–29 to 204°C); withstands short exposure to 600°F (316°C)
Pressure: max. 150 psi
Excellent mechanical, chemical, and heat resistance
Well-suited for hot, fatty, and oily products
Poor serviceability in steam use
Especially good for hard vacuum service
Low gas permeability

Viton is a registered trademark of DuPont.

Pumps and Valves

4. The brewery has many different types of pumps. How do some common types work?

Pumps can be broadly split into two families: centrifugal pumps and positive displacement (PD) pumps. Most pumps of either type should not be allowed to run dry, or seal failure will result.

a. Centrifugal pumps, or velocity-based pumps, are the most common type in the brewery. They may be of sanitary or nonsanitary construction, may be mounted on a vertical or horizontal axis, and may be of virtually any size. Unlike PD pumps (such as rotary lobe and progressive cavity types), centrifugal pumps are able to deadhead, or pump against a closed system with no damage to the pump. *Figure 1.1* shows a stationary application, and *Figure 1.2* shows a cart-mounted pump with a variable-frequency drive to control motor speed.

b. A liquid ring seal pump looks similar to a centrifugal pump, but the intake and discharge are located on the face of the pump head casing. Ring pumps have the ability to pump in either direction and can handle a mixed stream of liquid and gas. This property makes them ideal for use as CIP return pumps. For proper operation, these pumps require close construction tolerances and are therefore more costly. Other advantages to

Figure 1.1. Stationary mounted centrifugal pump in a clean-in-place system.

Figure 1.2. Cart-mounted centrifugal pump with variable-frequency drive.

pumps of this type include their ability to self-prime and pump heavier solids, such as yeast. As discharge pressures build, the output flow rate drops rapidly; thus, they are best used with an unrestricted, open-return system (*Figure 1.3*).

Figure 1.3. Self-priming liquid ring pump used for clean-in-place return.

Centrifugal pump theory and operation will be discussed in greater detail in the sections that follow.

PD pumps are characterized by an ability to generate constant flow rates across a wide range of discharge pressures. Because of this, most PD pumps should not pump against a restricted system, such as discharge with a closed valve, because they can easily develop pressures that will blow the end off a hose. The exception is the air diaphragm pump described below. Most PD pumps have the ability to self-prime.

c. Rotary lobe pumps operate by moving two carefully machined impellers closely past one another, creating an exceptionally smooth flow. Applications for these pumps include pumping heavy solids like yeast slurries or gentle, precise, low-shear transfers such as beer supply to a bottle filler (*Figure 1.4*).

d. Progressing cavity pumps move a helical impeller inside a specially shaped rubber stator. They are able to pump a wide variety of materials in a very gentle manner (including whole fruit!). Common applications in the brewery include pumping spent grain discharge and heavy yeast solids.

e. Diaphragm pumps are often used for chemical transfer applications. The common air-actuated double-diaphragm type can run dry and has the ability to deadhead to a user-controlled discharge pressure. As

Figure 1.4. Rotary lobe positive displacement pump used for pumping yeast and beer.

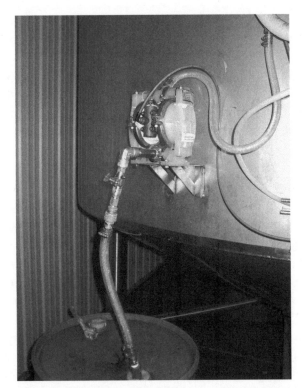

Figure 1.5. Air-driven double-diaphragm pump used for injection of chemicals.

such, they may be found in very small breweries supplying beer to a bottle filler. Internal seals must be carefully inspected to assure complete cleaning and sanitation when used for beer applications. These pumps are often used for chemical injection and sometimes for high viscosity applications such as removal of spent yeast or whirlpool trub (*Figure 1.5*).

f. Piston pumps are commonly seen in small-scale chemical feed applications. They are inexpensive and easily adjusted to deliver a varying quantity per stroke. These pumps are often used where high head pressure is required, such as boiler treatment feed applications (*Figure 1.6*).

g. Peristaltic pumps, or hose pumps, operate by rotating a roller along a hose, thus pushing liquid through the pump (*Figure 1.7*). Unlike other types of pumps, the moving parts never contact the product, making them highly sanitary. Thus, they are often used in laboratory and pharmaceutical applications. They are well suited for many dosing applications, such as chemical, yeast, finings, or diatomaceous earth. Additionally, peristaltic pumps can run dry without deleterious effect.

5. How does a centrifugal pump move liquid?

Centrifugal pumps consist of four main components:

a. An **impeller,** which spins and imparts rotational motion to the liquid
b. A **pump head,** which houses the impeller and the liquid
c. A **motor,** which powers the pump
d. A **seal,** which prevents liquid from leaking where the rotating motor shaft passes into the pump head

Liquid, allowed to flow into the center of the pump head casing, is acted upon by a rotating impeller that attempts to force it to the outer areas of the pump head. Force manifests itself on the liquid in two main forms: the liquid can be accelerated, resulting in flow, and/or the liquid experiences an increase in pressure.

As a rule, centrifugal pumps with slow impeller speeds and large casings are preferred for gentle wort and beer transfers. To minimize cavitation, transfers of very hot liquids or liquids that may have entrained gases also benefit from slow impeller speeds. Water movement, CIP supply, and high-pressure applications are commonly performed by pumps with high impeller speeds.

Figure 1.6. Twin-mounted alternating piston pumps for high-pressure steam boiler feed.

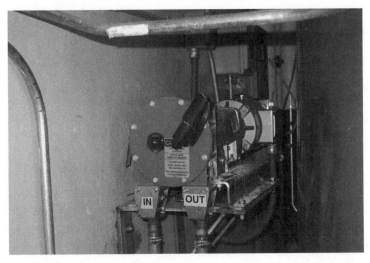

Figure 1.7. Peristaltic pump (hose pump) used for injecting fining material into the beer stream.

6. What is a pump curve?

When run at a constant speed, every pump discharges liquid with a combination of pressure and flow rate that can be described by a curve. A pump curve is a graph that shows this relationship and should be used when sizing pumps for a particular duty. These curves are often shown as defined for conditions of 60°F (15.5°C) water with a motor speed of 3,450 or 1,725 rpm. Under the predicated conditions, the pump always operates at some point on the curve. Pressure in centrifugal pumps is expressed in feet of head. This pressure is equal to the height to which a column of water would be raised. For reference, 34 feet of head is equal in pressure to 1 bar or 14.9 psi.

If downstream flow is halted, such as by closing a valve, the flow rate drops to 0 and the pump will both develop its maximum head and experience its lowest power consumption. Likewise, if no discharge restriction is present, the operational point moves to the far right of the pump curve.

The following information also is often shown on a pump curve:

> Power required for operation
> Efficiency of the pumping operation
> Effect of different impeller sizes
> Net positive suction head (NPSH)

As pumping factors change, the pump curves will likewise change. Temperature, viscosity, density, and flow characteristics are commonly examined in correctly sizing a pump to a given application.

7. What are the effects of varying the speed of the impeller in a centrifugal pump?

As motor (and thus impeller) speed changes, the curve experiences a number of predictable changes, sometimes called affinity factors. As the speed changes,

> the flow rate varies by the ratio of the change to the first power;
> the head varies by the ratio of the change to the second power;
> the power requirement varies by the ratio of the change to the third power.

Example. A 1,725-rpm pump at its maximum efficiency point uses 0.5 hp to develop 20 feet of head and generate a flow of 20 gallons per minute (gpm). If the impeller speed is doubled to 3,450 rpm, conditions at maximum efficiency are

flow rate	$20 \text{ gpm} \times (3{,}450/1{,}750)^1 = 20 \times 2^1 = 40 \text{ gpm}$
head	$20 \text{ ft} \times (3{,}450/1{,}750)^2 = 20 \times 2^2 = 80 \text{ ft}$
power	$0.5 \text{ hp} \times (3{,}450/1{,}750)^3 = 0.5 \times 2^3 = 4 \text{ hp}$

8. What is cavitation, and what are its negative effects?

Cavitation is the result of vapor bubbles forming and collapsing inside the pump head. This generally occurs on the trailing edge of the rotating impeller and sounds like marbles or gravel in the liquid being pumped. As the vapor bubbles collapse, small sonic booms are created, which physically erode the surface of the impeller and can cause premature seal and bearing failure in the pump. Because this is in essence a boiling action, as temperature and impeller speed increase, so does the possibility of cavitation. Restricting the outflow of the pump can help to minimize cavitation by increasing discharge pressure, thus moving the operational point to the left on the pump curve. One problem area where cavitation is often seen is in whirlpool operation at small breweries. The combination of high liquid temperature and low discharge pressure is particularly problematic; some breweries have found that adjustable VFDs (variable-frequency drives) on the pump motor can help solve this problem.

NPSH is a measure of the pressure required to prevent cavitation of the pump. The calculations for this value include many factors, but the most important one for many breweries is the frictional loss in the hose or pipe work supplying the pump. If the inlet piping to the pump restricts flow, the pump is said to be "starved," and cavitation occurs, both decreasing the pump's performance and contributing to eventual mechanical failure. For these reasons, it is good brewery practice to oversupply pump inlets. Putting elbows, valves, and tees in front of the pump inlet should be avoided, and adequate head pressure should be supplied by placing the pump close to or under the tank to be emptied.

9. How does a centrifugal pump seal work, and what happens when the seal fails?

There are two main areas that must be sealed on a centrifugal pump. The first is the outer casing to the backplate. A large O-ring gasket is usually used. The second and more difficult seal is between a rotating shaft and a stationary backplate. Mechanical seals are used in the brewery for this application and function by allowing a very thin layer of liquid to act as a lubricant between the seal faces. Rotating seals may be located inside or outside the pump head. While inexpensive pumps may contain a seal consisting of a Teflon O-ring riding on the stainless steel backplate, in better pumps very hard materials such as silicon carbide machined and polished to close tolerances are used.

One important fact to remember is that the liquid pressure at the center of the impeller is only as great as it is in the supply hose or piping. Because these seals are located in this low-pressure area of the pump head, there is the strong probability of significant oxygen ingress into the pumped liquid when they fail. Seals should be inspected for damage and wear on a regularly scheduled basis to assure high product quality. Flushing the seal with water can improve its performance by assuring that abrasive materials are not present in the thin lubrication layer. Such water-flushed double mechanical seals are often used for hot wort applications. Likewise, water-flushed single seals are used on CIP pumps to minimize chemical buildup.

One useful technique to check for leaking seals is to sample dissolved oxygen (DO) both upstream and downstream of a suspected leak. Because seals more readily pull air into the system than leak product out, elevated DO levels are symptomatic of such a leak. Temporarily cascading water over the seal should reduce DO levels.

10. The brewery has valves in many applications; what are some common types used?

The following valves are commonly used in breweries:

a. Butterfly valves are relatively inexpensive and sanitary valves, mainly suitable for on-off operation. The design of the butterfly valve features a disk that pivots on a center axis and is sealed with a replaceable valve seat of an appropriate electrometric material. This design allows for the complete cleaning of all product contact surfaces in a CIP operation when fully opened. Valves of this type are not recommended for incremental flow control, because they generate high shear in the product. Butterfly valves can be specified with lockout features (*Figure 1.8*).

b. Ball valves contain a rotating ball with a hole formed through the center to control flow. They are especially prevalent in gas distribution and water-piping applications. They are not considered sanitary in design for product use; salespersons claiming them as such should be questioned. These valves are generally inexpensive, long lived, and suitable for high-pressure applications. They are very good for on-off functions but not for regulating flow (*Figure 1.9*).

c. Globe valves are excellent at controlling flow. Operationally, a sealing disk controls the restriction of the flow path. Globe valves are often found in steam and water applications and are generally non-sanitary in design (*Figure 1.10*).

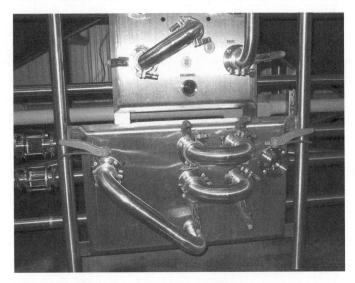

Figure 1.8. Butterfly valves on a swing panel.

Figure 1.9. Ball valves on supply piping to water pumps.

    d. Gate valves interrupt flow by moving a rigid gate across the liquid flow. Gate valves are inexpensive and should be used only for on-off, non-sanitary applications rather than flow control. Large models are used for spent grain applications in breweries.

    e. Solenoid valves are on-off valves that are actuated by energizing a small electromagnetic coil. When activated, the coil allows a diaphragm

Figure 1.10. Globe valves used to control the flow of steam to the brew kettle.

Figure 1.11. Brass solenoid valve used to control the flow of glycol to the tank jacket.

Figure 1.12. Diaphragm valve used to control flow of discharge from a pump.

Figure 1.13. Angle-seat plug valves used in a small keg washer-racker.

to move, thus permitting fluid flow. They are often used for glycol control and small pneumatic control duties (*Figure 1.11*).

    f. **Diaphragm valves** are used for sanitary, manual flow control (*Figure 1.12*). As a flexible diaphragm is raised, increasing flow is permitted.

Figure 1.14. Pneumatic actuator on a butterfly valve on a tank outlet.

g. Mix-proof matrix valves are both very sanitary and very expensive and are not usually found in small breweries. They are generally installed in a matrix of piping and, when closed, act as a block-and-bleed set, so that if a single seal were to fail, liquid would leak to the valve exterior, not into the connecting pipe.

h. Plug valves are an older style of valve still in use in sample cocks in many breweries. Disassembly is required for proper cleaning.

i. Angle-seat valves are structurally similar to globe valves but are pneumatically actuated for on-off operation. They are used in kegging equipment (*Figure 1.13*) and for similar applications.

11. What are some common ways of actuating valves?

a. Manual operation with a lever handle is the simplest form of actuation for valves.

b. In **pneumatic actuators,** compressed air is used to produce a rotational force. These actuators may close by allowing a spring to return the valve to home position (air open, spring close) or may be air powered in both directions (air open, air close) (*Figure 1.14*).

c. In **motorized actuators,** a motor is used, as the name implies, to provide the rotational force required to change valve position.

d. Valve positioners are a class of actuators that can open a valve by a variable and controllable amount to modulate flow (*Figure 1.15*). A

Figure 1.15. Valve positioner, modulating the opening of a valve according to a signal received from a temperature probe. This type of valve is commonly used for water or coolant mixing.

valve positioner matches the position of a valve to a control signal. Valve positioners are also known as "I-to-P" pneumatic actuator packages.

12. What is block-and-bleed?

Block-and-bleed is a valve and piping arrangement that allows for the closure of a hose or piping route by closing two in-line valves and opening a drain or vent valve between the two closed valves. In a sanitary brewery system, this configuration can be designed for use with multiple butterfly valves or through the use of a specialized double seat valve. This system can separate two process flows without the possibility of intermixing them as a result of valve leakage. These systems are often installed where CIP supply services interface with product flow.

13. How is resistance to flow through pipes and fittings calculated?

Specialized tables for fluid flow have been developed and can be consulted to determine the pressure drop liquid experiences as it flows at various speeds. When these tables are used, it is important to determine if the liquid flow is turbulent or laminar in nature. As a rule, all beer and water flow in brewery pipes is turbulent. The viscosity of the fluid is also

Table 1.1. Recommended fluid velocities

Item	Rate (ft/sec)
CIP (detergent)	10
Water	10–12
Wort	7–8
Beer	5
Mash to pump	5
Mash discharge	5–7
Yeast	3.3

required information for these calculations. Some fluids, such as yeast, have specialized, nonlinear viscosity characteristics. Yeast is thixotropic, which means that its viscosity drops when it is in motion (ketchup behaves similarly). For valves, the flow coefficient (Cv), a simplified system that represents resistance to flow, has been developed. It is defined as the flow rate of water at 60°F through a valve when acted on by a force of 1 psi (measured in gpm). The larger the Cv value, the less resistance to flow.

14. How fast should fluids flow through pipes in a brewery?

Many different types of fluids move through pipes in the brewery, and the maximum recommended flow rates for these fluids vary widely. Gentle transfer of beer and wort is essential for reasons of product quality; very rapid transfers can cause shear stresses that destroy hot break, promote excessive fountaining and foaming, or draw a vortex into the product as it is removed from a tank. For cleaning applications, the mechanical action of a rapid, turbulent flow assists with cleaning of the pipe interior. Excessive water, gas, or steam flow rates can cause significant pressure drops through the affected system, resulting in insufficient supply of these services. Recommended flow rates for the brewery are listed in *Table 1.1.*

15. How is flow rate calculated?

Flow rate is a measure of volume moved over time. Volume of media transferred per unit of time divided by cross-sectional area of the pipe results in fluid velocity.

Example.   Beer in a brew pub is flowing at 0.5 bbl/min through 1½-in. tubing. What is the fluid velocity in the pipe?

If the tubing is standard sanitary stainless steel, measured by its outside diameter, with a wall thickness of 0.065 in., the cross-sectional area of the tube is

Table 1.2. Flow rates through sanitary tubing of various sizes

Pipe size (tubing OD, in.)	Gallons per minute at flow velocity of:		
	5 ft/s	7 ft/s	10 ft/s
1.5	27.50	38.6	36.75
2.0	49.00	68.6	98.00
2.5	76.50	107.25	153.20
3.0	110.00	154.4	220.60
4.0	196.00	274.5	392.20

$$\pi r^2 = 3.14 \times \left(\frac{1.5}{2} - 0.065 \right)^2 = 1.474 \text{ in.}^2$$

The flow rate of the beer is

$$0.5 \text{ bbl/min} \times 31 \text{ gal/bbl} \times 231 \text{ in.}^3/\text{gal} = 3581 \text{ in.}^3/\text{min}$$

The velocity of the beer is

$$\frac{3581 \text{ in.}^3/\text{min}}{1.474 \text{ in.}^2} \times \frac{1 \text{ min}}{60 \text{ s}} \times \frac{1 \text{ ft}}{12 \text{ in.}} = 3.37 \text{ ft/s}$$

Flow rates through sanitary tubing of various sizes are given in *Table 1.2*.

16. How is the volume of a tank calculated?

Tanks are generally constructed in the basic geomantic shapes of cylinders, cones, and hemispherical heads. Most brewery heads are of the standard flanged and dished (F+D) type. Volumes for these can be found in tables available online from vendors such as Paul Muller Co. or Enerfab.

Geometric volumes are determined by the following formulas:

$$\text{volume of a cylinder} \quad V = \pi r^2 h$$

$$\text{volume of a cone} \qquad V = \pi r^2 h/3$$

in which

    V = volume
    r = radius of the base of the cylinder or cone
    h = axial length of the cylinder or cone

The following conversion factors are useful in calculating the volume of a tank:

    1 gallon = 0.13368 ft^3 = 231 in.^{3}
    1 liter = 1,000 cm^3

Heating and Cooling

17. What are some ways that heat may be introduced into the brewhouse?

Although steam is by far the most applied method of imparting heat to brewing operations, other heat transfer methods used include direct-fire gas, electric immersion elements, microwave transmitters, and even pressurized hot water. Heat can be measured in British thermal units (BTU), which is the amount of heat required to raise 1 pound of water by 1 degree Fahrenheit. This heat rise is specifically defined as from 63 to 64°F (17.2 to 17.8°C).

18. Why is steam so widely used in brewery applications?

Steam has the capacity to deliver a large amount of heat quickly to a point of use without the need for additional pumping. As a pound of steam condenses to water at a pressure of 15 psig, it transfers 946 BTU of energy. This is the amount of energy required to raise 5.25 pounds of liquid water from the freezing point to the boiling point, a rise of some 180 degrees Fahrenheit. The flow of steam is relatively easy to control, and it is one of the most efficient ways to cleanly transfer BTUs locked inside fossil fuels to the brewing process; in fact, it is more efficient than heating the kettle with direct fire. In addition, the relatively low temperature at which the transfer occurs causes less thermal stress on the wort and reduces the danger of scorching.

19. How does a steam boiler operate?

Fossil fuels are burned in a boiler designed to promote an efficient transfer of heat from the flame to water. The boiling point of water changes with pressure; as the pressure increases, so does the boiling point. As we know, at sea level water boils at 212°F. At 15 pounds of pressure (psig), the boiling point of water is 250°F, and at 50 psig it is 298°F. As the water is heated, it boils, giving off steam. As more steam is created, the pressure in the boiler increases until an upper operational pressure is reached and the fuel supply is interrupted. When the pressure in the system reaches a lower operational pressure set-point, the fuel supply is restarted. Boilers that operate at pressures below 15 psig are considered low-pressure boilers and are subject to fewer regulations than high-pressure boilers. As heat is required in the brewery, steam valves are opened and steam flows to heat transfer surfaces. The steam gives up its heat and condenses back into water. This condensate is returned to the boiler either by pressure or through a condensate pump return system to begin the cycle again.

Various configurations are used in boiler design and construction. After being ignited and combusted, the heated gas transfers its heat to boiler water. The construction of the boiler may be such that the gases flow around a set of cast sectional plates or an assembly of tubing bundles. These bundles route either the boiler water or the combustion gases. Some small, low-pressure boilers may be designed as "atmospheric" draft units, in which the combustion of gases occurs directly under the heat transfer surfaces and the exhaust moves upward through the flue stack by convection. Larger or high-pressure units that force combustion air into the combustion chamber are called forced-draft systems. The boiler is equipped with safety systems such as an upper pressure safety switch, low water cutoff, flame sensors to prevent fuel flow without combustion, and a mechanical pressure relief valve.

Steam generators are specialized boilers sometimes used breweries. They merit special mention because of specific operational concerns. Steam generators introduce small volumes of water into the heat transfer bundle, where it is quickly vaporized into steam. Because of the small volumes, these units start up and build steam very rapidly but are also prone to scale buildup and corrosive attack. Special attention must be given to chemically treating makeup and return water to steam generators.

20. How is the size of a boiler measured?

Boilers are sized according to the amount of heat that they can transfer. Boilers operate at 80–85% efficiency. Small breweries are generally equipped with steam boilers sized to produce 50,000 BTU per barrel of brewhouse capacity. Thus, for a brewery with a brew length of 10 barrels, a boiler sized for 600,000 BTU/hr of input energy is standard and actually produces about 486,000 BTU/hr at an efficiency of 81%. Boiler horsepower is an alternative measure of size (1 hp = 33,000 BTU/hr). Natural gas is a common fuel used for boiler operation; when burned, it releases about 1,000 BTU/ft^3.

21. Besides the boiler, what other components are used in steam systems in breweries?

Steam systems may be simple or complex. Other components of steam systems may include the following:

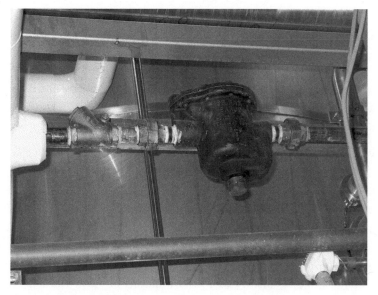

Figure 1.16. Bucket steam trap, commonly used for separation of steam and condensate.

a. A **steam header** collects steam from the boiler and routes it to branching supply pipes.

b. A **drip leg** separates out condensate before it can enter steam valves. Condensed water droplets impacting steam control valves can cause damage or erosion.

c. **Isolation and control valves** restrict or direct steam to where it is needed.

d. Steam traps keep steam in the heat transfer area by allowing only the passage of condensed steam. Many different types are in use; the most commonly used in breweries are the floating thermostatic (F + T) traps and inverted bucket traps (*Figure 1.16*).

e. Strainers are placed upstream of traps to prevent blockage or fouling. Both strainers and steam traps should be serviced and cleaned yearly.

f. A **condensate return pump system** moves condensate back to the boiler location. It may be powered by steam pressure or be an electrically operated centrifugal pump and collection tank.

g. Back-check valves prevent condensate from flowing backward in the system.

h. The **boiler feed tank** stores and may even deaerate condensate and makeup water until it is called for by the boiler controls. The associated boiler feed pump pushes the water into the boiler as needed.

i. The **blowdown tank** reduces the temperature of boiler blowdown to a level acceptable for discharge into the drain system during regular blowdowns.

22. What maintenance concerns should be addressed for the steam system?

Steam boilers and supply piping can be subject to substantial and costly corrosion and pitting. The primary causes are dissolved O_2 and CO_2 gases. In addition, scale and sludge can build up in the boiler heat transfer areas. The most common method of protecting this expensive and vital equipment is a well-monitored water treatment program. In addition to feeding the boiler with very soft water, development of a chemical addition program with a competent boiler water treatment specialist is the best method of mitigating the worst effects of corrosion. Regular blowdown of the boiler is also critical; most should be blown down every day they are used. Regular testing of the CO_2 content in the stack gas is an important tool to maximize efficiency. Finally, proper monitoring of boiler operation and condensate composition cannot be overemphasized; boilers should be drained and inspected on a yearly basis. Steam traps should be regularly inspected and cleaned.

23. What are the heating power requirements for brewhouse operations?

The brewhouse is the single largest user of heat energy in most small breweries. Boiler efficiency, insulation efficiency, peak loading, and other factors should be considered for actual operations. At first assessment, most small breweries seem to have oversized boiler systems. However, the variable nature of the small brewery operation coupled with the small incremental capital cost justifies this increased capacity. The figure of 50,000 BTU/bbl of brewhouse capacity mentioned previously allows for multiple simultaneous operations. Some rough calculations of heating requirements for individual operations are shown below.

Example 1. Wort boiling in the kettle. For 1 bbl of wort boiling in the kettle, evaporating at a rate of 5% per hour during boiling, the heating power required can be calculated as follows (the latent heat of vaporization for water at 1 atmosphere of pressure is 970 BTU/lb):

$$1 \text{ bbl} \times 31 \text{ gal/bbl} \times 8.34 \text{ lb/gal} \times 0.05 \text{ evaporation/hr} \times 970 \text{ BTU/lb}$$
$$= 12,539 \text{ BTU/hr}$$

Example 2. Wort heating in the kettle prior to boiling. For 1 bbl of wort to be heated from 150 to 212°F over a period of 1 hr, the heating power required can be calculated as follows:

1 bbl × 31 gal/bbl × 8.34 lb/gal × (212°F − 150°F)/hr × 1 BTU/°F
  = 16,030 BTU/hr

These calculations are greatly simplified. A greater level of detail in the calculation of heating loads and other engineering topics can be found in the recognized brewing literature.

24. What are primary and secondary coolant systems, and where are they found in the brewery?

a. Primary coolant is refrigerant gas that is compressed, condensed, and evaporated to move heat in a mechanical system. This system uses electricity to power a compressor. Examples of refrigerant gases in common use include ammonia, used in large breweries, and the Freon family of refrigerants.

Although ammonia is a more efficient and environmentally benign refrigerant gas than Freon, it is not as common in the small brewing industry for both safety and service reasons. Ammonia is a powerful respiratory irritant and in sufficient quantities can cause death. Government regulations mandate safety equipment and proper training of workers in plants with ammonia-based cooling. To be cost effective, a refrigeration load greater than 200 hp is generally required. Many refrigeration service contractors are not equipped to work on such systems, often resulting in higher service costs. *Figure 1.17* shows a 50-hp ammonia compressor.

Freon systems, although less efficient, are very common in small-scale cooling applications, such as home air conditioning and restaurant refrigeration. There are a number of different formulations that comprise this group of refrigerants. Although all these gases have been identified as greenhouse gases, some are more benign than others. Members of this class include R-502, R-22, and the more environmentally responsible modern refrigerants R-404A, 134A, and 401A (a direct replacement for the discontinued R-12), which is also known as MP-39.

b. Secondary coolant is cooled by the primary coolant and is normally circulated in the plant to handle process cooling loads. Secondary coolants include food-grade propylene glycol or less commonly a brine

Figure 1.17. Ammonia reciprocating compressor used to chill propylene glycol.

solution. These solutions have high heat removal and retention properties, are less prone to leaks than refrigerant gases, are nontoxic in the event of unintended mixing with brewery products, are relatively easy to control, and can be held at a temperature that prevents unwanted freezing of beer on heat transfer surfaces. Because glycol is expensive and can carry less heat than water, the solution strength is of importance. A mixture of 33% glycol and 67% water is considered appropriate for a standard system operating at 26°F (–3.3°C). Solution strength can be easily checked with a temperature-corrected hydrometer. Maximum operational efficiency of a glycol system is obtained by not running the glycol any colder than necessary. Glycol temperatures should be set at or slightly below the freezing temperature of beer, 29°F (–1.7°C). Recovering and using any heat created by the refrigeration cycle through the use of a system such as a Thermastor is also cost effective.

25. How does the refrigeration cycle work?

The refrigerant is held in a receiver as a liquid at near ambient temperature. The pressure that it is under varies with the refrigerant type; for 404A, it is about 225 psi.

When cooling is required, an expansion valve opens and allows refrigerant to flow through a small orifice from the receiver to the evaporator.

The evaporator functions as a heat exchanger. The refrigerant undergoes a drop in pressure and changes phase from a liquid at near ambient temperature to a low-pressure gas. As the liquid evaporates into a gaseous state, the physical laws that govern the behavior of gases require that the temperature drops. Heat is then able to be absorbed from the secondary cooling medium. The low-side pressure in a 404A system is about 60 psi.

The compressor is a mechanical device that compresses the now cool, lower-pressure gas. The same physical laws that demand heat uptake in evaporation now necessitate a rise in temperature as the gas is raised in pressure.

The hot, high-pressure gas now flows to a condenser, which may resemble a large automotive radiator. Here in the cooling coils, the gas gives up heat and condenses back into a near ambient temperature liquid. The refrigeration cycle is now complete.

26. What are the different types of refrigeration compressors?

Most of the compressors in use in small breweries are of the piston type and operate by allowing refrigerant gas to fill a cylinder when its associated piston is retracted. As the piston moves inward and reduces the volume of the cylinder, the gas is compressed. Small piston compressors (up to 10 hp) may be of the hermetically sealed "coffee can" type, which are also commonly found in household and automotive refrigeration applications. Both the motor and compressor in this type are completely sealed in a housing. Somewhat larger compressors, which can resemble an automobile engine in appearance, also operate on the piston principle. Screw compressors are generally larger still and more efficient and operate without the characteristic hammering sound of the piston type.

27. What other ancillary equipment may be associated with a refrigeration system?

a. **Compound gauges** are used by refrigeration service technicians to read high-side and low-side pressure simultaneously as an aid in diagnostic functions. Additional refrigerant may also be added by using this equipment.

b. Liquid line dryers remove water from the refrigerant as it is fed to the expansion valve. Water, which is noncompressible, can quickly damage a compressor. To monitor the effectiveness of moisture removal, a sight glass is often installed adjacent to the dryer.

c. Suction accumulators are gas reservoirs placed just upstream of the compressor.

d. Oil separators prevent refrigeration oil from entering the compressor. Oil, like water, is noncompressible, and excessive amounts in the compressor can present problems.

e. A **hot-gas bypass valve** may be installed to allow the compressor to run at reduced load and prevent excessive starting and stopping of the compressor.

f. Water-cooling towers may be used in addition to or instead of air-cooled condenser coils.

28. How is the size of a cooling system measured?

Refrigeration size can be described by input power or heat rejection capabilities. One often-quoted conversion factor for refrigeration is that 1 ton of cooling = 1 brake hp input power = 12,000 BTU/hr removed. In general, as the difference between the ambient temperature and the desired refrigeration temperature increases, the system loses efficiency. A call to the manufacturer can reveal that equipment of 10-hp input size may be capable of providing only 6 tons of cooling at a specified temperature.

29. What is the magnitude of cooling loads in the brewery?

The largest loads on brewery cooling systems deal with cooling wort to fermentation temperature, controlling fermentation, cooling the beer to conditioning or packaging temperatures, and heat gains through tank and pipe insulation. Typically, breweries utilize a cold liquor tank or ice bank as an energy storage device to distribute the large loads associated with wort cooling over a longer time span, thus spreading the cooling demand and reducing the maximum cooling power requirements.

Example 1.   For wort cooling in the summer using municipal water chilled in a heat exchanger and stored in a cold liquor tank, assuming that the water is delivered to the cold liquor tank heat exchanger at 76°F (24.4°C) and must be cooled to 42°F (5.6°C) over 4 hours for use in the wort heat exchanger to reach a pitching temperature of 52°F (11.1°C). The ratio of water used to wort cooled is 1:1.1 by volume:

$$1\,\mathrm{bbl}\times1.1\times31\,\mathrm{gal/bbl}\times8.34\,\mathrm{lb/gal}\times\frac{76°\mathrm{F}-52°\mathrm{F}}{4\,\mathrm{hr}}\times1\,\mathrm{BTU/°F}$$

$$=17{,}064\,\mathrm{BTU/hr}$$

Example 2. Similar equations are used to calculate product cooling to conditioning or packaging temperatures, although the specific heat of beer differs from that of water slightly. The rough calculation for chilling beer with a specific gravity of 1.012 (3°P) from an ale fermentation temperature of 68°F (20°C) to a filtration temperature of 30°F (–1.1°C) is as follows (time for this chilling operation is not specified):

$$1\,\mathrm{bbl}\times1.012\times31\,\mathrm{gal/bbl}\times8.34\,\mathrm{lb/gal}\times(68°\mathrm{F}-30°\mathrm{F})\times1\,\mathrm{BTU/°F}$$
$$=9{,}942\,\mathrm{BTU}$$

Example 3. Fermenting beer releases about 560 BTU/bbl for every degree Plato of apparent fermentation drop. If beer ferments at a rate of 2.5°P per day, to maintain temperature it presents a chilling load of

$$1\,\mathrm{bbl}\times2.5°\mathrm{P/day}\times560\,\mathrm{BTU/°P/bbl}\times1\,\mathrm{day/24\,hr}=58.3\,\mathrm{BTU/hr}$$

Example 4. The calculations dealing with heat flux through an insulated wall are beyond the scope of this work. However, for a point of reference, a 30°F (–1.1°C) tank with an R-value of 6 in a 70°F (21.1°C) room fluxes roughly 6.5 BTU/hr/ft^2.

30. What maintenance should be performed on refrigeration systems?

Refrigeration systems, like all other critical equipment, should be examined regularly to assure proper, efficient operation. These examinations should be scheduled at least annually, and service paperwork should be filed for later reference. Semiannual maintenance at the change of seasons is recommended for critical equipment.

One of the most damaging conditions for refrigeration equipment is short-cycling. Because the compressor is controlled on the basis of system pressures, insufficient refrigerant in the system can cause the compressor to start and stop at short intervals. Compressors, like automobile engines, experience the greatest wear during the starting process.

The cooling coils on the condenser require cleaning at regular intervals. The coils should be cleaned at least once a year, although equipment, demand, and local conditions may require more frequent cleaning. Airborne plant material, such as cottonwood, can be particularly problematic for air-cooled condenser coils.

31. What are the expected operational pressures for Freon systems?

Knowing operational pressures is important for troubleshooting problems with refrigeration systems. Permanently installed gauges can be found on some systems; acceptable pressures should be posted adjacent to such gauges for this purpose. For systems running on R-22, R-502, and R-404A, evaporator pressures of 50–65 psi are common. Although pressures vary at ambient temperatures, normal operational pressure in the condenser should be 225–275 psi for these refrigerants. For the gases R-12, MP-39, and 134A, pressures should be 20–30 psi for evaporators and 125–165 psi for condensers.

Compressed Gases

32. How is carbon dioxide stored at the brewery?

Carbon dioxide is used extensively for cellaring, packaging, and dispense operations in the craft brewery. In large brewery operations, CO_2 is collected from fermentation, purified and compressed, stored, and used for brewery needs. In small breweries, it is generally delivered and stored as a bulk liquid at approximately 250–300 psi and –10°F (–12.2°C) in an on-site bulk tank. Bulk tank options include the relatively small 600-lb vacuum-insulated Dewar tanks and the larger, mechanically refrigerated storage tanks with 4–60 tons of capacity. For draft dispense or particularly for small volume applications, nonrefrigerated compressed gas cylinders of up a 50-lb capacity are available. These cylinders are not generally used for normal brewery purposes because they are not economical.

CO_2 is withdrawn from the tank as required, and the pressure is reduced to brewery requirements. As is the case with all liquefied or compressed gases, the temperature falls as it vaporizes or expands in volume. At high flow requirements, this physical factor can cause supply problems because delivery and regulation systems may ice up. Pressure builders, which are located at the storage tank, and vaporizers help prevent supply problems. Vaporizers may be of a passive, radiator type or can be active, with heat applied from steam or an electrical heating element. Pressure regulators are available in many sizes; large models can both handle greater flows and resist icing.

33. What is compressed air used for in the brewery?

Compressed air is used in a number of situations in the brewery, including many mechanical operations in the packaging hall, actuation of valves, wort aeration, and evacuation of tanks and CIP lines. Pneumatic point loads are generally small because performing mechanical work with compressed air as a power source is quite inefficient and thus the relative cost of use is very high. Compressed air applications take advantage of its high degree of controllability, low cost of routing, and ease of safety lockout procedure. Compressed air is generally supplied at 90–120 psi and reduced to working pressure at the point of use.

34. What are some common compressor types used in the brewery?

Air compressors are in many ways similar to liquid pumps: they operate on a velocity-based principle, like that of a centrifugal pump, or on the positive displacement model. Many compressor options are available, including oil lubricated or oil free, the number of compression stages, cooling method, and motor drive type. Compressors for industrial applications operate at pressures of 100–125 psi and are sized by horsepower. At these pressures, 1 hp delivers approximately 4 standard cubic feet per minute (SCFM).

Positive displacement compressors take in air and mechanically reduce the space occupied to increase pressure. Reciprocating piston compressors are the simplest, least efficient, and least expensive compressors available. Rotary screw compressors rotate two intermeshed helical screws past one another and are similar to a lobe pump in operation. Unlike the piston-based compressors, they offer an air supply free of pressure pulses.

Impellers are used in rotary centrifugal compressors to transfer pressure to the air. This type of compressor is oil free by design and is usually the most expensive option. They are generally designed for applications where high purity or high capacity is demanded.

35. What additional equipment is associated with the compressed air system?

a. Dryers remove moisture from the air supply. As the air is compressed, humidity present naturally condenses. Water is condensed by chilling the air as it passes through the dryer. Liquid water in the compressed air supply can cause significant problems for pneumatically powered equipment. Dryers are generally installed adjacent to the compressor.

b. Storage tanks are used to increase peak capacity, acting as buffers by holding compressed air. Wet air tanks are installed upstream of the dryer, while dry air tanks contain air treated for use. In addition, tanks can be installed close to the point of use to compensate for small supply lines to deal with intermittent, high-volume loads.

c. Distribution piping for compressed air systems can be constructed of aluminum, copper, steel, or stainless steel. Air hose and poly tubing are acceptable for short runs from regulators to equipment. PVC is not acceptable; it is susceptible to shattering and presents a safety hazard. Piping concerns include both leaks and excessive pressure drops caused by undersized piping runs. It is estimated that a single small leak in a threaded fitting costs $65 per year.

d. Filters can be found throughout the compressed air system. They may be required to filter out contaminates in air exiting the compressor or at individual points of use. Filters can be purchased for specific duties, such as oil removal or sterile filtration.

e. Oilers feed lubrication into the air supply and are installed at the point of use. Some pneumatic equipment, such as actuated pistons, benefits from an air supply containing a small quantity of oil.

Electrical Systems

36. What is the theory behind electrical systems?

A *circuit* is a closed conducting path or route consisting of resistors and conductors through which an electric current travels. *Conductors* are any materials that support the flow of electrons. In a circuit, the wires that carry current are considered the conductors for that circuit. Anything that resists the flow of electrons is termed a resistor. Resistors in brewery circuits convert electron flow into heat, light, or motion. Insulators are substances with resistance high enough to prevent the flow of electrons. Plastic, rubber, glass, and porcelain are all excellent insulators. The *voltage source* provides the electron supply for a circuit. It might be the 350,000,000-watt power company generator or your watch battery.

The basic unit of electrical potential is the *volt* (V). This potential can be higher than, lower than, or equal to the electrical potential of the earth at a given location, which is referred to as *ground*. The flow rate of electrons as they move through a system is measured in *amps* (A). Resistance to electron flow is expressed in *ohms* (Ω). Electrical flow in a circuit can be calculated by using simple formulae; the fundamental law of electricity is known as Ohm's law, which states that it takes 1 volt to move 1 amp through 1 ohm of resistance: $V = A \cdot \Omega$. The power law, $W = AV$, reveals that the power, measured in watts, used in a device is equal to the current in amps times the voltage. Since volts are defined by Ohm's law, the power equation can also be written as $W = \Omega A^2$.

Using the power equation to analyze a common 120-V circuit powering a 60-W light bulb, one can determine the total current flowing through that circuit. The power equation can be rewritten as $A = W/V$. Thus, the bulb would be using 60/120 or 0.5 A of current. A 120-W light bulb would likewise use 1 A of current and would produce a glow twice as bright by using twice as many amps. Applying Ohm's law, $V = A\Omega$ or $\Omega = V/A$, the resistance of such a bulb would thus be 120 ohms. In a circuit where the resistance approaches zero, the resultant amperage flowing through the circuit becomes very large. A circuit of this type is termed a *dead short* and can be created by touching a live wire directly to ground with no intermediate load.

37. What are inductive and resistive loads?

Electrical loads can be thought of as primarily resistive or inductive in nature. In resistive devices, such as toasters, water heaters, and incandescent light bulbs, electrical force is used to produce heat or light. Inductive devices take advantage of the fact that, as fundamental forces of nature, electricity and magnetism are linked. When current exists in a length of wire, the wire radiates lines of magnetic force. If the wire is coiled, the forces are concentrated. If a conductor crosses magnetic lines of force, then an electrical potential in that conductor is induced. Induction is the basis of operation for transformers, motors, and generators and can be generated by an expanding and contracting magnetic field or by the movement of the conductor through the field. The operation of a generator or alternator involves developing a magnetic field in a coil of wire and cutting that field by turning a second coil of wire to induce electrical potential. The physical force that turns the coil may be provided by water moving through turbines at the Hoover Dam or a belt attached to the engine of a car. A motor can be thought of as the reverse of a generator or alternator; a motor uses electricity to develop physical motion.

We can think of an electrical circuit as the flow of electrons from a point of electrical potential through wires and switches past a load, returning to the point of electrical potential. If the flow of electrons is in only one direction, that circuit is a direct current (DC) circuit. Nikola Tesla realized that it was possible to significantly reduce power transmission losses by reversing the direction of the flow of electrons periodically. The frequency at which the current alternates is measured in cycles per second, or hertz (Hz). Alternating current (AC) is supplied at 60 Hz in the United States, while 50 Hz is the standard in Europe. AC power can be easily changed from a high voltage/low amperage supply to a low voltage/ high amperage supply or vice versa. This operation occurs in a transformer. Transformers are rated by line voltage (power in), load voltage (power out), and capacity. The capacity of a transformer is given in volt-amps (VA), which is simply the product of volts times amps; 1 kilovolt-amp (kVA) is equal to 1,000 VA.

38. What is grounding, and why is it important?

The National Electric Code (NEC) provides standards for installation of electrical circuits and assures that the transmission and use of electricity are safe. The most important concept for safety in electrical use is grounding. If a wire were to break or work loose inside an electrical device, it could cause the exterior of the device to have electrical potential. An operator touching such a device could provide an electrical path to ground through his body, possibly resulting in severe injury or even death. Grounding provides a ready path to ground for any stray electricity. All circuits and devices should be properly grounded to provide a safe work environment.

39. What is the difference between single-phase and three-phase electricity?

Standard household current in the United States is supplied at 110 V AC. If a circuit is powered with two 110-V AC wires cycling 180° out of phase with each other, the electrical potential across any load is 220 V AC. Points of high energy use, such as an electric water heater, dryer, or stove, use 220-V power sources to lower the amperage draw. One or two wires containing electrical potential are used in single-phase systems. Three-phase systems have three hot wires, also known as legs, supplying current 120° out of phase. Residential 110/220-V electrical service commonly consists of two out-of-phase hot wires, a common wire, and a ground wire.

The common wire is used to complete the circuit for 110-V service. Both the common wire and ground should have an electrical potential of 0 relative to each other and to earth ground. Three-phase systems can come in many varieties of voltage and configuration. The most common supply for small users is 208 V in a Wye configuration. Other voltages often encountered are 230 and 460. Some facilities may have more than one type of three-phase power available.

40. Why are the wires inside an electrical panel different sizes and colors?

Copper wire covered with colored insulation is commonly used as a conductor in electrical circuits. Wire is sized by gauge; the smaller the gauge, the larger the wire. The NEC specifies what types and sizes of wires may be used for a given electrical load. For example, according to the NEC, 12-gauge wire is the smallest wire allowed to carry 20 amps of current.

The voltage of the power supplied can be listed in a multitude of ways. At a facility, 110-V power may start from the point of transformation at 115 or 120 V and experience a voltage drop of 4% or more. Thus, 110-, 115-, and 120-V power are all basically the same. The color of wire used acts as a visual code and should tell something about the voltage range that is carried. The hot wires in 110/220-V single-phase and 230-V three-phase circuits are black, red, and blue. The hot wires in 460-V circuits are brown, orange, and yellow. The common wire is white. Green and uninsulated wires are reserved for ground. Red wires are also commonly found as control wires inside an electrical panel. European three-phase equipment generally uses blue, black, and brown for wires with electrical potential; green is reserved for ground wires.

Low-voltage power, such as 12- or 24-V supply, is inherently safer than 110-V or higher voltages and as such is used for low-power applications, such as phone lines, stereo speakers, and very small motors. Because it is inherently safer, the NEC allows less rigorous precautions for its use. For example, the use of low-voltage power in fermenter temperature control can both reduce the cost of installation and increase the safety of such a system.

41. What is the NEMA 4 standard?

The National Electrical Manufacturers Association (NEMA) sets standards for electrical equipment. NEMA 4 is a waterproof standard for the construction and installation of equipment, defined as "protection against hose-directed water." Other standards include general purpose, dust-tight, and industrial standards. In general, brewers should specify the NEMA 4 standard in all process areas.

42. How does a brewery's electrical control panel work?

A circuit is simply a complete electrical path from a source of electrical potential through conductors (wires) and load(s) back to the source. DC and AC circuits operate the same way, so it is often easiest to visualize the flow of electrons in only one direction. In an example of a very simple circuit, electrons flow from a battery through a switch and a bulb and back to the battery. In more complex circuits, other devices may be used to control, regulate, and utilize power. These devices can be schematically depicted on an electrical drawing to provide a map for the operator or electrician. One common method of drawing such circuits is the ladder line diagram. On it, electricity is represented as being supplied down the left side and flowing left to right through controls and loads to a common line on the right side. As long as a complete and unobstructed path exists from the power source through devices and back to the power source, electricity will flow. In actuality, the panel built from such a drawing looks nothing like the diagram. However, having such a map is very useful for diagnosing circuit problems. Diagrams should be stored inside control panels for easy reference.

43. What are some common items found in brewery electrical systems?

a. Switches are the valves of electrical wiring. One confusing fact about switches is that while a valve allows flow when it is open, an open switch prevents electrical transmission. Switches may control flow along multiple paths in multiple directions. A single-pole single-throw (SPST) switch either allows or prevents flow from one point to another. A double-pole switch has two electrical routes, i.e., two distinct switch paths controlled by a single toggle. A double-throw device switches power from a single inlet between two outputs. Switches may be actuated by a variety of means. One popular type is the momentary pushbutton. This switch changes position only as long as it is pushed. The switch controlled may be normally open (NO) or normally closed (NC).

b. A **relay** is a special type of electrically operated switch. Small relays are used widely in control wiring and many resemble small, clear plastic cubes mounted on a connection base. These "ice cube relays" allow the automation of many processes in the brewery. Relays are switched by supplying them with a small amount of power. When power is supplied, the switches in the relay change position: NC paths are opened and NO paths close.

c. The **main disconnect switch** is one of the first things to look for in any panel. This switch de-energizes the entire panel. The NEC requires that all electrical loads be outfitted with some sort of disconnect in close proximity and line of sight. For a panel, this is usually a switch that prevents power from being turned on if the panel door is open. Remember that the line (power-in) side of the switch is still energized when the switch is in the off position.

d. Fuses are important and common safety elements used in electrical control. Fuses prevent dangerous quantities of electricity from moving through a circuit, protecting both equipment and people. In the event of a dead short, the resistance of a circuit drops to near zero and the amperage attempts to significantly increase. In such a circuit, the only resistance is provided by the wires, and they begin to heat up, potentially starting a fire. Fuses are designed such that a maximum quantity of amperage is allowed to pass before they open, thus preventing further flow. Many electrical loads require high amperage to start and then quickly settle down to a lower operating range. Dual-element or time-delay fuses allow current flow of five times rated capacity to exist for up to 10 seconds before they open. Regardless of its time delay, if a dangerous short occurs in a circuit protected by a dual-element fuse, it will open nearly instantaneously.

e. Heaters are placed in a circuit to monitor and arrest amp flow if it exceeds a defined quantity. Heaters are sized to match the load they are protecting. As power flows through the heater, it passes through a bimetallic assembly. Resistance in the unit produces heat and causes the metals to expand at different rates. The heater opens the circuit when a set point is exceeded. Commonly, the set point can be adjusted to different capacities within a given range. If a heater is set at 5.7 A and the motor it supplies begins to pull 6.5 A, the heater opens, preventing the motor from overheating and burning out. Before a heater is reset, it first needs to cool down. A properly adjusted heater that continues to trip signals that the motor is attempting to do more than it was designed for or that some internal failure may be causing the motor to overheat.

f. Circuit breakers are similar to heaters. They protect entire circuits and are found in the main electrical control panel. Breakers provide circuit protection against both short circuits (instantaneous large amp draws) and slight overcurrent events. In the case of an amp draw of 40 times rated capacity, a circuit breaker will open in as little as 0.016 seconds. Smaller overcurrent values may take up to 5 minutes to trip the breaker. One special type of breaker is the ground fault interrupter (GFI). It monitors current, and if there is a difference of current flow between a hot wire and the common wire, it opens the circuit very quickly. These breakers are required in all bathrooms in new construction and should be used in the brewery to link and protect 120-V outlets in wet areas and near sinks.

g. A **motor starter** is used to control and protect an individual motor. The starter is an assembly combining a heater and a contactor, which is basically a heavy-duty relay. A small amount of power is supplied to an internal coil, which causes a multipole switch to close rapidly. The energy that flows through the switch is used to power the controlled motor. These devices may be used to switch large electrical loads, because they are designed to prevent arcing at the switch contact points. Most contactors have additional switched contacts to provide control or display functions.

44. What is a latching circuit?

One of the most common and useful circuits found in the brewery is the latching, or holding, circuit. This circuit is energized when the start switch is depressed and remains so until the stop button is pushed or a fault disengages the circuit. The circuit is held open by energy powering the contactor coil, which passes through the additional points on the contactor. One advantage to using these circuits is that they allow the use of safer, lower-voltage power to control large electrical loads. A common latching circuit contains an NO switch for motor start and an NC switch for motor stop.

45. How do electric motors operate?

Motors use electrical induction to develop mechanical power (physical motion). Most motors used in breweries today are of the AC type. Large-duty equipment, such as a pump, is commonly powered by three-phase power. Three-phase power is both more efficient (more motion with less electrical usage) and has a smaller amp draw for a given size motor, which allows for smaller conductors when wiring.

Most common motors found in the brewery consist of a rotor, a stator, bearings, and some type of housing. The rotor has a number of metal bars arranged parallel to a central shaft upon which it rotates. The stator surrounds the rotor and contains coils known as windings, which produce a rotating magnetic field when power is applied. As the magnetic field rotates, it cuts across the metal bars of the rotor and induces voltage in those bars, which in turn produce a magnetic field in the rotor core. The magnetic field in the rotor interacts with the stator magnetic field to produce the twisting effect called torque. In a motor of this type, the rotor turns at a speed slightly slower than the speed of the rotating magnetic field. The speed at which the rotor field rotates is set by the frequency of the electric source and the configuration of the windings. In the case of a common two-pole configuration, the speed of the field is equal to the frequency of the electrical source. Power in the United States is supplied at 60 cycles per second, and there are 60 seconds in a minute. Thus, the field in a common two-pole motor turns at 3,600 rpm. The speed at which the rotor lags behind the stator field is referred to as slip and for motors of this type is 2–6%. Common listed motor speeds are 3,450, 1,725, and 860 rpm.

Many motors are wired in a multitap arrangement that allows the windings to be connected in different configurations, allowing different voltage supplies to be used. Common multitap motors have one configuration for 208 or 230 V and a separate configuration for 460 V. Regardless of the type of motor, the electrical connections are made inside the peckerhead.

The stator of a three-phase motor has three single-phase windings. The direction of rotation is determined by the arrival sequence of power in the windings. If the phases are arriving as A-B-C, the motor spins in one direction. Switching any two phases causes the motor to spin in reverse; by switching B and C, power arrives as A-C-B, which is A-C-B-A, or simply C-B-A.

Single-phase motors have two sets of windings, the starting windings and the running windings. The starting windings develop a strong torque to assist in getting the motor turning. A capacitor, a device that functions like a battery, stores additional electricity that is used to help power the starting windings. As the motor achieves operating speed, a centrifugal switch deactivates the starting windings. By switching the leads of the starting windings, the direction in which the motor will be started, and thus run, can be reversed. A single-phase motor can often be recognized by the characteristic hump of the capacitor on its side. Single-phase motors can fail because of problems involving the capacitor. The capacitor can short circuit if the motor is started and stopped frequently in a short span of time. Therefore, motors of this type should be started and stopped no more than 20 times per hour.

46. How can the speed of a motor can be controlled?

Both single- and three-phase motors run at a single, predetermined speed. This speed is dependent on the frequency (in hertz) of the electricity that powers the motor. The development of the AC inverter, or variable-frequency drive (VFD), has revolutionized motor control by providing an affordable and reliable means of managing speed. VFDs work by taking the supplied AC power and rectifying it to a DC form. The DC power is stored temporarily in capacitors, and the inverter reconstructs an alternating current, sinusoidal waveform at user-specified frequencies between 0 and 120 Hz. Drives are limited by the maximum amount of power that they can handle and are commonly sized by maximum horsepower rating. Use of a VFD is limited to three-phase motors. One additional advantage to using a VFD is that no contactor or heaters are required to protect the controlled motor because the VFD itself monitors and protects the unit. In general, VFDs are excellent for controlling devices such as pumps and mixers.

Using a VFD to control a motor can cause premature motor failure if the motor is incorrectly specified for the application. The cause of this motor failure is excessive heat buildup in the motor resulting from insufficient cooling. Most motors are cooled by rear-mounted fans. Operating the motor at low speeds dramatically reduces the volume and velocity of the cooling air supplied. A standard motor powering a variable torque application, such as a centrifugal pump or fan, should be able to successfully operate through a 10:1 turndown ratio. Turndown ratio is defined as the ratio of the motor's rated speed to its operational speed. For a 60-Hz base application, a 10:1 ratio allows operation between 6 and 60 Hz supplied to the motor. For a constant torque application, like a conveyor, 4:1 turndown is allowable. More difficult applications require the use of special motors rated for inverter duty, some of which can successfully operate in a 100:1 turndown ratio duty.

47. What important information can be found on a motor nameplate?

a. Frame.   Describes the physical size of the motor itself. This information is used primarily for finding a replacement that will fit the application.

b. Type.   Refers to the manner in which the motor is sealed or enclosed. Open drip-proof (ODP) motors can allow moisture to enter the windings and bearings and should not be used in wet environments. Most brewery application pump motors are of the totally enclosed fancooled (TEFC) type. Washdown duty motors can be built as TEFC or totally enclosed nonventilated (TENV) types with special seals, paints, gaskets, and stainless shafts for very wet environments. Explosion-proof motors can be totally sealed so that sparking inside the motor housing does not ignite an explosion. Obviously, mill motors should always be of this type.

c. Volts.   The voltage rating refers to how much power should be applied to the motor for proper operation. In many motors, the windings are arranged so that different voltages can be used; a 208-230/460 motor can be wired for 208- or 230-V service or configured for 460-V service. Most small industrial motors are constructed in this split-wound configuration.

d. Amps.   The amperage rating specifies how many amps are required to power the motor at its rated horsepower. In a 1-hp split-wound motor, this may be listed as 4.0-3.6/1.8, where 4.0 is the ampacity for a 208-V application and 3.6 is for a 230-V application. A motor supplied with 460 V requires only 1.8 A for operation.

e. Phase.   Specifies whether single- or three-phase power is required for operation of the motor.

f. Rotations per minute (RPM).   Speed at which the motor turns when all other nameplate conditions are met.

g. Horsepower (hp).   The maximum horsepower the motor is rated to deliver.

h. Efficiency.   How efficient the motor is at converting electrical energy into mechanical motion.

i. Ambient.   The temperature environment in which the motor is built to operate.

j. Duty.   Continuous-duty motors can safely operate fully loaded 24 hours per day. Intermediate motors require time to cool down between uses.

k. Service factor.   A measure of how much power can be drawn from a motor in relation to its rated capacity. A 2-hp motor with a service factor of 1.15 can actually deliver 2.30 hp of motion. It is not wise to regularly run a motor in the service factor range. The service factor can be thought of as reserve capacity.

48. Why do motors fail?

If you work in any industrial setting long enough, sooner or later you will find yourself with a motor that does not run. Motors go bad for many reasons, so understanding what causes them to fail can help to prevent premature failure. One of the main reasons for motor failure is excessive heat. All motors need to dissipate the heat generated during operation. In a TEFC motor, a small fan attached to the rotor shaft blows air on the motor casing. Operating such a motor in a tight, enclosed space at a low electrical frequency or in an excessively warm environment may not allow the fan to cool the motor sufficiently to prevent the insulation separating the windings from overheating and failing. Excessive heat can also cause internal soldered connections to melt. One particularly damaging event for three-phase motors occurs when one or more legs become de-energized, shifting the entire load to the remaining legs. This phasing can quickly overheat a motor and cause serious damage. Properly sized heaters protect a motor from this event.

All motors have bearing surfaces, and if they are not properly lubricated, the forces of friction can create excessive heat in the motor and cause bearing failure or overheating. Running a motor above its rated load can also cause it to overheat. In general, better motors have more durable windings that allow for better heat dissipation. Cheap motors are generally built less robustly and can burn out faster. Oversizing a motor may prolong its life in particularly problematic duties. Remember that the machine that the motor is powering, not the motor itself, determines how much energy will be used for a given application. A 3-hp motor attached to a pump with a load of 1 hp will consume just 1 hp of energy to move product.

Another cause of motor failure is a dead short, which can occur between two of the windings or a winding and the case or when one winding breaks internally through vibration or other means. In general, motors tend to fail shortly after installation because of a manufacturing defect or they overheat and fail. Obviously, the abundant quantities of water in use in a brewery can also cause motor problems. Water is an excellent conductor of electricity and so it can cause problems with any circuit it gets into. Water can enter a pump through faulty bearings or an unsealed housing. To prevent water problems, only TEFC or washdown duty motors should be used in wet areas.

Table 1.3. Multimeter use guide

Property to be tested	Units	Points to be tested	Uses
Voltage	Volts	Live circuit or to ensure that circuit is off	Live circuit confirmation Testing voltage of circuits
Resistance	Ohms	Dead circuit	Fuse testing Testing for short circuits
Current	Amps	Live circuit	Motor load testing

49. What is a multimeter?

Regardless of what type of electrical problem is encountered in the brewery, the most valuable tool for diagnosing a problem is probably the multimeter. It allows fast, accurate readings to be made, is inexpensive, and can prevent accidents when properly used. A multimeter, as the name suggests, is a combination meter used to measure many electrical variables. A multimeter should be able to measure voltage (both AC and DC), resistance, and low levels of current, measured in milliamps. *Table 1.3* lists uses of multimeters.

a. The **voltmeter** function is used to determine whether a voltage potential exists between two points and is used by touching the tool leads to the points.

b. The **ohmmeter** is used to measure resistance. The ohmmeter is always used on a de-energized circuit. It is used to test fuses (zero resistance indicates that the fuse is good; infinite resistance indicates that the fuse is blown) and to check for short circuits.

c. The **ammeter** measures how much current is passing a given point. The best type for brewery work is the clamp-style ammeter attachment. When this type of attachment is used, the circular clamp is opened and placed around the wire to be tested. The test is noninvasive and can easily read a large current flow while the wire remains safely covered with insulation. Tests of this type can determine whether a pump is pulling more amps than the motor was designed for or whether a chiller is running efficiently.

Process Controls

50. What is process control?

Process control is a term that refers to a broad group of automation, control, monitoring, supervision, and optimization issues affecting processes such as brewing or packaging beer. Process control utilizes instruments such as sensors to gather information and devices such as pumps and valves to control the affected process, often automatically. Automated functioning can manage systems as simple as a single temperature controller or as complex as a computer-driven, multilevel, integrated packaging operation.

51. What are programmable logic controllers, and what do they do?

Typically, small breweries utilize processes with a high degree of direct operator control: brewhouse valves are opened manually and pumps are started and stopped directly by the brewer. However, more small, inexpensive, and powerful programmable logic controllers (PLCs) are being installed in many pieces of equipment within the brewery. PLCs were developed to emulate hard-wired control circuitry by utilizing "relay logic." Signals from input devices are processed within the PLC, and an output signal is produced to control external devices. These simple, fast, reliable, and rugged industrial computers are often programmed by using "ladder logic," which visually resembles the wiring diagram for a hard-wired electrical system performing the same duty. Operator interface with a PLC, although not required, may be done through a human machine interface (HMI) as simple as a start/stop button or as complex as multiple networked personal computers. Increasing sophistication of external devices has given rise to complex device protocols such as the Fieldbus remote I/O.

52. What is the difference between discrete and analog control?

Discrete control refers to a binary state (on-off) type of control. In analog control, continuously variable quantities such as voltage or pressure are utilized. A motor starter is a discrete control: it is either on or off. A VFD can regulate a motor to a variety of speeds and is thus considered an analog in nature.

The most common analog signal standard used in the brewery is the 4- to 20-ma (milliamp) standard. A current flow varying between 4 and 20 ma is carried on an 8- to 28-V DC circuit. Devices that utilize this standard may transmit, process, or receive these signals to indicate values or control other devices. Examples include instruments, sensors, process controllers, motors, and valves.

Sensors that utilize this standard include instruments that signal measurements of physical states such as weight, pressure, flow rate, temperature, speed, and level by allowing a current flow proportional to the range of the instrument. Controlled devices can include variably opening valves and VFDs. For example, a pressure transmitter (PT) with a span of 0–100 psi will pass 4 ma at 0 psi, 20 ma at 100 psi, and 12 ma at 50 psi. Likewise, a VFD controlled by 4- to 20-ma current will run at half-speed when presented with a 12-ma current.

Generally, 4- to 20-ma control requires the use of a process controller. Manufacturers make a wide range of controllers that take a 4- to 20-ma signal input from an instrument (such as a PT), scale it to engineering units (such as psi or atmospheres), perform operations based on that signal (such as dampening), and then output the resultant 4- to 20-ma signal to the controlled device (such as a VFD or valve positioner).

Humans are able to anticipate an end result and thus can intuitively modulate a control factor. One example of this is the reduction of pressure on an automobile's gas pedal as a desired speed is approached. This anticipatory control can be emulated through the proportional-integral-derivative (PID) algorithm, which can prevent wide swings of the controlled state by automatically adjusting a control variable to hold a process variable at a set-point. PID "loops," for example, vary the speed of a pump to control the pressure in a glycol supply system as it approaches a given set point, thus preventing an overshoot of the desired value.

53. What are some common instrumentation devices found in breweries, and how do they operate?

a. Level indicators.
Discrete devices include the following:

1. Reed-style float switches operate when a magnetic switch is triggered by a float sliding over a shaft.

2. Optical switches use the difference in refractive index to trigger a state change.

3. Liquid level conductivity probes are triggered when liquid conducts a small electric current between two metal rods.

4. Tuning fork switches utilize the difference in resistance to vibration between liquids and gases (such as air). They are particularly effective in harsh environments, such as CIP tanks.

Analog level indicators include the following:

1. Float switches, in which a float moves past a resistive probe, are commonly found in beer filler bowls.

2. Capacitance level measurement uses an immersed electrode and measures the capacitance of the changing level of the fluid media. The capacitance is converted to a current charge proportional to the level of the measured media.

3. Time-in-flight (TIF) devices measure the distance to a liquid surface by using ultrasonic, radar, or sonar waves. These devices are expensive and are not commonly used in small breweries.

b. Flowmeters/totalizers

1. Mag meters generate a magnetic field through which a conductive liquid is routed. The liquid induces an electric current, the magnitude of which is proportional to the speed at which the liquid is flowing through the device. These are rugged yet simple and sanitary devices with no moving parts and are ideal for many flow measurement duties in the brewery (*Figure 1.18*).

2. Coriolis meters, or mass meters, measure the mass of the media moving through the meter by measuring how much the flow tube is twisted as liquid flows through it. These meters are highly accurate but more expensive than mag meters.

3. Vortex shedding meters operate by disrupting the flow path of the media with an obstruction; sensors downstream measure the vortices to gauge the magnitude of flow. They are excellent for the measurement of media such as steam.

4. Turbine meters are actuated as pressure from the flowing liquid acts on the vanes of a turbine immersed in the media. The rate of spin is proportional to the rate of flow. Turbine meters are commonly of nonsanitary design, are relatively inexpensive, and find excellent use as water flow rate/flow totalizers in small brewery applications.

5. Rotameters have a freely moving ball trapped within a tapered clear tube. Liquid or gas flow causes the ball to move upward, and the meter is read visually. These are very inexpensive devices.

c. Pressure instruments

1. In most simple pressure indicators and switches in breweries, a Bourdon tube is used as a measuring element. This is a coiled tube that flexes and attempts to straighten out as pressure is applied to it. Small levers and gears indicate pressure on a gauge or actuate a switch.

Figure 1.18. Magnetic flowmeter with display, used to measure flow rates.

2. In pressure transmitters, the capacitance principle is used to make data available for process control. These instruments can be built to sanitary standards for inline use.

3. Differential pressure transmitters are sometimes found on lauter tuns to indicate bed compaction. They also operate on the capacitance principle.

d. Temperature indicators

1. Bimetallic temperature indicators and switches utilize the principle that different metals expand at different rates as they are heated. The internal action is similar to that of Bourdon tube pressure indicators.

2. Glass thermometers are useful for visual indication but are fragile and not easily used for process control.

3. Thermocouples are joined pairs of dissimilar metal wires and generate a low voltage at their junction, proportional to the temperature difference between the ends. The two most common thermocouple

Figure 1.19. Photoelectric eyes mounted on packaging equipment used to detect case cartons. Cartons block a light beam and send a signal to the programmable logic controller.

alloys for brewery use are iron-constantan (type J) and Chromel-Alumel (type K).

4. In a resistance temperature detector (RTD), the principle that the electrical resistance of metals increases with temperature is used. Although RTDs have a higher cost than thermocouples, their advantages include superior linearity and a higher signal-to-noise ratio. RTD systems, particularly those with three or four wires, can sense temperatures very accurately over long transmission distances.

e. Photoelectric eyes, proximity switches, and microswitches. These devices are used extensively in the bottling hall. Proximity switches are also used in the brewhouse to sense valve position.

1. Photoelectric eyes (PE) operate by bouncing a beam of polarized light off a reflector. Disruption of the beam causes an internal switch to change states (*Figure 1.19*).

2. Proximity switches (*Figure 1.20*) used in the brewery generally are of the inductive type. They generate an electromagnetic field that is affected when a metal object passes close to the face. Nonmetallic objects can be sensed by capacitive proximity sensors, but these devices are easily triggered by water and therefore are not commonly found in the brewery environment.

Figure 1.20. Proximity switches used to detect proper flow path on a swing panel. The metal extension rod makes contact with the switch to complete the circuit.

3. Microswitches are small electrical switches triggered by physical action. They are of a simple, rugged design.

f. Dissolved oxygen (DO) meters. As a liquid such as beer moves past a membrane, oxygen moves through the membrane and is consumed in an electrochemical reduction reaction. The current generated as this takes place is amplified, measured, and converted to a value that corresponds to the oxygen level measured. DO can be measured with portable meters or with inline instruments, which are permanently mounted in the process stream.

g. Load cells. Load cells are electronic weight measurement devices that can be mounted directly to process equipment (*Figures 1.21* and *1.22*). The load cell consists of a strain gauge bonded to a metal support. As the metal is stressed by the mass applied, the strain gauge changes resistance. This change in resistance is then scaled and converted into a digital weight value.

Figure 1.21. Tank legs mounted on load cells for measuring the weight of the tank contents. The load cells transmit a signal to a controller that can open and close the tank outlet valve for batch weighing.

Figure 1.22. Tank hanging from load cells.

54. What is a P&ID, and how is one read?

A piping and instrumentation diagram (P&ID) is a drawing or set of drawings that describes a process such as brewing. It is useful for project management, troubleshooting, and the development of standard operating procedures. A P&ID is intended to be a detailed schematic of a process, and as such equipment should be represented simply and symbolically. These drawings should include process vessels, other heat transfer equipment, pumps, essential valves, controls such as pressure regulators, permanent instruments, and sensors such as flow meters and temperature sensors. Equipment and especially valves and pumps should be labeled clearly on both the P&ID and in the field. Piping sizes and flow directions should also be designated. A legend to the symbols and abbreviations used should be provided. *Figure 2.5,* Volume 3, shows an example detailing a CIP system. Most P&IDs conform to a standard set of drawing symbols and abbreviations; for example, instruments are drawn as circles, with their function identified by a letter code.

MORE INFORMATION ON TOPICS DISCUSSED IN THIS CHAPTER

Numerous abbreviations for standards and standards-regulating organizations are used in brewery engineering. A few of the common ones are

ANSI   American National Standards Institute
ASME   American Society of Mechanical Engineers
BSP   British Standard Pipe Thread
DIN   Deutsches Institut für Normung
GHT   Garden Hose Thread
ISA   Instrument Society of America
ISO   International Standards Organization
NEC   National Electric Code
NEMA   National Electrical Manufacturers Association
NPT   National Pipe Thread

REFERENCES

Alerich, W. N., and Keljik, J. 2001. *Electricity 3: Power Generation and Delivery.* Delmar Learning, Clifton Park, N.Y.

Alerich, W. N., and Keljik, J. 2001. *Electricity 4: AC/DC Motors, Controls, and Maintenance.* Delmar Learning, Clifton Park, N.Y.

Alfa Laval. *Alfa Laval Pump Handbook.* www.alfalaval.com

Crane Co. 1988. *Flow of Fluids Through Valves, Fittings, and Pipe.* Technical Paper 410. www.craneco.com/flow_fluids.cfm

Glover, T. J. 2000. *Pocket Ref.* Sequoia Publishing, Littleton, Colo.

Heald, C. C., ed. *Cameron Hydraulic Data.* www.flowserve.com/pumps/

Hoffman Specialty. *Steam Traps Engineering Data Manual.* Hoffman Specialty, ITT Fluid Technology, Chicago.

Holle, S. R. 2003. *A Handbook of Basic Brewing Calculations.* Master Brewers Association of the Americas, St. Paul, Minn.

Kubla, T. 2001. *Electricity 1: Devices, Circuits and Materials.* Delmar Learning, Clifton Park, N.Y.

Kubla, T. 2001. *Electricity 2: Devices, Circuits and Materials.* Delmar Learning, Clifton Park, N.Y.

Kunze, W. 1996. *Technology Brewing and Malting.* International ed. Versuchs- und Lehranstalt für Brauerei, Berlin.

Larson, James. 1989. Fundamentals of fluid flow. (Class material.) Siebel Institute of Technology, Chicago.

McCabe, J. T., ed. 1999. *The Practical Brewer: A Manual for the Brewing Industry.* 3rd ed. Master Brewers Association of the Americas, Wauwatosa, Wisc.

Rainbow, C., and Float, G. E. S., eds. 1983. *An Introduction to Brewing Science and Technology.* Institute of Brewing, London.

Spirax Sarco. 1991. *Design of Fluid Systems Steam Utilization.* Spirax Sarco, Cheltenham, U.K.

Swihart, M. S. 1997. Healthy beer transfers: A review of sound brewing practice and design. *Technical Quarterly of the Master Brewers Association of the Americas* 34(2): 107–114.

Syska, R. E., and Birk, J. R. 1980. *Pump Engineering Manual.* Flowserve Corporation, Dayton, Ohio. www.flowserve.com

Waukesha Cherry-Burrell. 1992. *Waukesha Pumps Engineering Manual.* Waukesha Cherry-Burrell, Delavan, Wisc.

INTERNET SOURCES

www.plasticstechnology.com/articles/200403fa3.html
www.pfonline.com/articles/059905.html
www.pfonline.com/articles/119806.html
www.thermastor.com
www.engineeringtoolbox.com

CHAPTER 2

Plant Sanitation

Ashton Lewis

Springfield Brewing Company
Paul Mueller Company

1. What is sanitation?

The word *sanitary* is derived from the Latin *sanitas,* or "health." In general, sanitation is the actions taken to ensure a healthy or hygienic environment. Brewery sanitation, then, is the sum of all tasks required to create a healthful and hygienic environment in the brewery.

2. Why is brewery sanitation important?

Beer is a product of controlled fermentation using particular yeast strains (and sometimes bacteria of particular genera). Proper sanitation allows the brewer to control the brewery environment and maintain microbiological control of the beer. Failures in brewery sanitation can result in contaminated and spoiled beer.

Sanitation is also important because it protects brewery equipment. Proper cleaning removes organic and inorganic soils (for example, trub and beer stone, respectively) that could lead to corrosion in crevices in equipment.

Finally, beer is a food product and, like all foods, must be produced in accordance with good manufacturing practices.

3. What pest control is commonly needed in breweries?

The most fundamental brewery sanitation practice is good housekeeping, primarily measures to combat pests. The most common pests in small breweries are fruit flies, houseflies, rodents, and insects associated with malt, such as weevils and beetles. Good housekeeping and plant design are very effective in reducing pest problems. Common-sense sanitation practices include

a. Routine cleaning of floor drains and floors
b. Sweeping or vacuuming spilled grain from the grain storage floor
c. Installation of door sweeps on outside doors to minimize the gap under them
d. Installation of screens on windows
e. Minimizing the length of time when doors are left open
f. Storing bags of malt and other ingredients on pallets
g. Contracting with a pest control company for routine service

The goal of housekeeping is the elimination of food and shelter that attract pests. Fruit flies, for example, are attracted by fermentation, especially of rotting fruit and spilled beer. These small flies are common around untidy bars and fermentation cellars.

Houseflies are minimized through general tidiness and barriers to their entry. Installing mesh screens and windscreens and keeping outside doors closed help to keep flies out of the brewery. Houseflies are attracted to ultraviolet light, and traps equipped with UV lights are effective in attracting and trapping flies that make it into the brewery. Unsanitary conditions that promote the breeding of flies can become a severe problem, because houseflies remain close to where they hatch, and one female can produce thousands of offspring during one breeding season.

Mice and rats are attracted to spilled malt, and if rodents are present in a brewery, they are usually in the malt room. Rodents can squeeze through very small openings. Rats can fit through an opening the size of a quarter, and mice can squeeze through an opening as small as a nickel. They seek shelter in warm places with an abundant source of food, especially as the outside temperature begins to drop in the fall and winter. Rodents are nocturnal animals, and they are creatures of habit, following routines in their movements. They typically use a common path between their nests and a food source and tend to follow walls. Traps are usually located adjacent to walls; bait stations are located outdoors only. Rodent droppings are a clear sign of these pests. When rodents are present in the brewery, swift action must be taken to eliminate them, since they carry disease and can quickly damage bags of malt.

Insects such as weevils and beetles can infest grain storage silos, conveyors, and mills and must be eliminated by using an approved fumigant

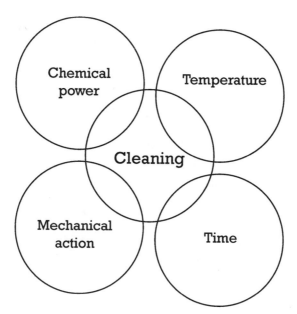

Figure 2.1. The four elements of cleaning.

after the malt has been removed. At many breweries, silos are regularly fumigated, to prevent economic losses from infestation of malt. Most pesticides and all fumigants are controlled materials and can be applied only by a licensed pest control operator contracted for these services (or a brewery employee who has had proper training and is licensed by your state).

4. What is cleaning?

Cleaning is the removal of soils from equipment. There are three general types of cleaning actions: mechanical, chemical, and thermal.

5. What considerations are taken into account in developing a cleaning strategy?

There are four key elements in the cleaning equation: the strength of chemical cleaners, the temperature of the cleaning solution, mechanical power, and time (*Figure 2.1*). Brewers can control the interaction among them. In general, increasing chemical strength, temperature, and mechanical input reduces cleaning time. However, limits on these inputs may be imposed by other factors, including safety, potential damage to equipment, and cost.

6. **What factors affect cleaning?**

Mechanical cleaning involves physical methods, such as scrubbing, spraying, and turbulence, to remove soils from equipment. Cleaning tools include brushes, abrasive pads, impingement spraying devices, and pumps. The most basic type of physical cleaning involves old-fashioned elbow grease and brushes and scrubbing pads for manual cleaning of brewing equipment. Tanks are usually cleaned with impingement spray devices, which produce high-velocity liquid sprays to blast soils from surfaces. Mechanical cleaning of transfer lines and hoses uses liquid turbulence to help scrub soils away.

Chemical cleaners assist in mechanical cleaning by dissolving and dispersing soils into the cleaning solution. Some spray devices do not rely on impingement but rather produce a thin film of water or a cleaning solution that cascades over the entire surface of the tank, cleaning without mechanical action. The thermal component of cleaning comes into play if the cleaning solution is heated to improve its dissolving power.

7. **What is sanitizing?**

Sanitizing reduces the number of microorganisms in an environment. The specific biological targets in the brewery are yeast and bacteria. It is important to distinguish between cleaning and sanitizing, since it is possible to reduce, and even eliminate, microbiological populations in an unclean environment. It is also possible, and quite common, for a clean piece of equipment to have living microorganisms on its surface.

8. **Why should equipment be cleaned before sanitizing?**

Many sanitizers lose their potency when applied to an unclean surface because they react with organic soils. Cleaning should always precede sanitizing, because the goal is to have clean, sanitized equipment.

9. **What is a sterile environment?**

A sterile environment is one that is completely devoid of life. Although the terms *sanitize* and *sterilize* are often used interchangeably, they do not mean the same thing. Sterilization techniques (for example, the use of steam in an autoclave or pressure cooker) are commonly used in the laboratory, but they are typically not used in the brewery. In special cases, equipment is sterilized and maintained in a sterile condition, for which the term *aseptic* is used. Aseptic processing is important in some sectors of the food industry, such as dairy and juice processing, and it is used in breweries for beers sold as shelf-stable products that do not require cold storage.

10. What is CIP?

Cleaning-in-place (CIP) is cleaning of equipment without disassembly or transport to a different location, such as a sink. The advantages of CIP include reduced labor, increased worker safety, and less equipment wear caused by disassembly and reassembly.

11. What is COP?

Cleaning-out-of-place (COP) is cleaning of equipment at a location removed from its point of use, typically after disassembly. COP is used when CIP is not effective.

12. What is sanitary design?

Sanitary design refers to methods of constructing equipment so that it can be effectively cleaned and used in food-processing applications. Key components of sanitary design include

a. Smooth surfaces
b. Absence of crevices and cracks
c. Absence of deadlegs in piping runs
d. Ability to bleed air from high spots in pipe runs that can trap air
e. Absence of cleaning shadows (areas not contacted by liquid sprays during cleaning) in tanks
f. Tanks designed to allow complete draining
g. Use of food-grade components

Equipment that inherently has crevices, such as plug valves, must be designed to allow disassembly. When equipment is designed for CIP, the term *sanitary design* takes on a broader sense, signifying that the equipment is actually clean after a CIP cycle.

13. What are sanitary standards?

Sanitary standards are design criteria developed to ensure that products are not contaminated during production and that processing equipment can be cleaned. Most sanitary standards are established through the collaboration of groups representing industry and groups or agencies representing public health. Numerous standards are currently used around the world, and most of the standards for the sanitary process industries have similar goals. Since most suppliers of sanitary processing equipment (for example, pumps, valves, in-line instrumentation, and vessels) compete in the global market, the number of commonly used and accepted standards is likely to decrease in the future.

14. What are 3-A standards?

Two industry groups, the Milk Industry Foundation and the International Association of Food Industry Suppliers, and a professional group, the International Association of Food, Milk and Environmental Sanitarians, collaborated in the 1920s to establish a standards organization that became known as 3-A. It is one of the oldest recognized standards organizations in the dairy and food industries.

The early goal of 3-A was to establish a uniform code for fittings used in dairy pipelines. Over time, 3-A standards covered all equipment designs used in the dairy industry. In 1944, the U.S. Public Health Service announced its official cooperation with 3-A, and today the U.S. Department of Agriculture is also represented on the 3-A standards committee.

It is important to remember that dairy products support the growth of pathogenic microorganisms, and the purpose of the sanitary standards followed by the dairy industry is to protect the public from contaminated products. Brewers who use the 3-A standards focus on those pertaining to good sanitary design and ease of cleaning, rather than on those relating to pathogens.

15. What are BPE standards?

The American Society of Mechanical Engineers (ASME) established the Bio-Processing Equipment (BPE) standards in the 1990s to address the special needs of the biopharmaceutical industry. Prior to the creation of these standards, the pharmaceutical industry relied heavily upon 3-A standards.

The ASME BPE standards have very detailed sections pertaining to orbital welding technique, material finish, stainless steel composition and mill lot tracing, weld inspection methodology, and the extremely important topic of documentation. Portions of the ASME BPE standards are applicable to the brewing industry, but many of the provisions are not relevant, because the concerns of the biopharmaceutical industry and the U.S. Food and Drug Administration are much different from the concerns of the brewing industry.

A helpful portion of the ASME BPE standards involves fitting size uniformity. For example, two sanitary tube elbows may carry the 3-A stamp and be functionally the same. However, this does not mean that the two elbows are the same size. The ASME BPE standards do cover fitting shape, because the orbital welding machines used to weld tubing and fittings together are much more sensitive to fitting shape and size than fittings hand-welded together. This means that all 2½-inch tube elbows carrying the BPE stamp are the same size and shape, making it easier for manufacturers and breweries with in-house welders to purchase identical parts from different manufacturers.

The ASME BPE standards, although developed in the United States for use by U.S. companies, have been recognized as international standards. In October 2002, a liaison to the BPE standards committee was formed with the Deutsches Institut für Normung (DIN) and the European Hygienic Engineering and Design Group (EHEDG). The application of the ASME BPE standards in other countries continues to grow, and they will be most likely to emerge as one of the most prominent set of standards used (in part or in their entirety) by the pharmaceutical and food industries.

16. What is a sanitary fitting?

Sanitary process systems can be joined together permanently by welding or temporarily by sanitary fittings. Temporary connections are preferred where disassembly for cleaning or maintenance is required or where impermanent arrangements of pumps, valves, and hoses (such as those used for racking) are needed. While numerous types of accepted sanitary fittings are used in breweries, all share certain traits.

Sanitary fittings are joined to form a junction that is crevice free, entirely composed of food-grade surfaces, and able to be cleaned. All commonly used fittings consist of two mating pieces held in place by a threaded connection (not in contact with the product) or a clamp, and most fittings rely upon a gasket to provide a seal between the mating pieces. Pipe thread connections are not sanitary, because of the inherent crevice created when a male pipe is threaded into a female pipe fitting, and because the threaded connection is in contact with the product.

17. What are some common sanitary fittings?

a. Clamped connections. Clamped connections generally involve an elastomer gasket and a clamping mechanism.

1. The **Tri-Clamp fitting** is the most commonly used sanitary fitting in small and medium-sized breweries. The Tri-Clamp trademark was originally owned by Ladish Tri-Clover and is now owned by the Alfa Laval group. This popular fitting is also manufactured by other companies and is commonly called a sanitary clamp connection. The fitting has two identical ferrules with flat faces, each containing a machined groove designed for an elastomer gasket that is sandwiched between the ferrules. A clamp is used to tighten the fitting, compressing the gasket to form a seal.

2. The **Swagelock TS series fitting** is a new style of fitting based on the sanitary clamp connection but designed to prevent over-tightening of the clamp and extrusion of the gasket into the product flow. The stainless steel ferrules have stops to limit the compression of the gasket and an oversized groove to accommodate enlargement of the gasket out of the product stream. The groove also captures the gasket and aligns the fitting. The TS series fitting is used primarily in the pharmaceutical industry and is limited in availability on stock items such as valves, pumps, and instruments. It is possible to join a standard sanitary clamp fitting to a TS series fitting if an adapter piece is used. The ease-of-use concerns are the same for the TS series fitting as for the standard sanitary clamp connection.

3. The **Waukesha Cherry-Burrell I-line fitting** consists of a female and a male ferrule that slip together for a self-aligning fit. A flat gasket is placed between the ferrules, and the connection is made with a clamp. The I-line fitting is most commonly used in high-pressure applications.

In practice, many brewers find clamped connections cumbersome, especially when dealing with difficult-to-handle parts, such as heavy valves and large hoses. Clamp connections are also extremely difficult to reconnect in emergency situations, such as accidental removal of a valve from a full, pressurized beer tank. This mistake occurs often enough that there seems to be a universally accepted remediation strategy: open the displaced valve, put the gasket in, and attempt to jam it back into place while a co-worker replaces the clamp. This method is not guaranteed to work, but it is guaranteed to soak the brewing staff with beer!

b. Threaded fittings. Threaded fittings have the same sanitary features as clamped fittings but use a nut to connect and tighten the fitting. The threads on the nut and the female portion of the fitting are not in contact with the product and do not present cleaning problems like those associated with threaded pipe connections.

One of the key advantages of threaded fittings is that they are difficult to disassemble when under pressure, because the line pressure tightens the nut against a landing used to tighten the nut into the fitting. Furthermore, if a threaded fitting is accidentally disconnected while in use, it is much easier to reconnect than a clamped fitting.

1. John Perry fittings are similar in design to the I-line fitting, except the female portion has threads on the outside and the male portion is tightened into place with a large hex nut. Since the nut slips over the male portion, John Perry fittings are similar to a pipe union and can be rotated without twisting the male and female fittings about the gasket.

2. DIN (or DN) sanitary fittings are also finding acceptance in U.S. breweries. These fittings have a part called the liner and nut (collectively forming the female assembly) and a male portion with a machined groove to capture and hold an elastomer O-ring gasket in place. The nut is smooth on the outside, with notches designed to fit a spanner wrench. DIN fittings can also be rotated without rotating the mating portions. These fittings are most commonly used on equipment manufactured in Europe, but they can be purchased in the United States. DIN fittings for use with tubing of U.S. sizes (with the diameter specified in inches as opposed to millimeters) conform to the DIN standard, but their tube ends are sized for butt welding with inch-sized tubing that can be mated with standard U.S. tubing.

3. SMS fittings are the Swedish equivalent of DIN fittings and are occasionally used on European equipment. The basic design is similar to that of DIN fittings, but the thread sizes and the physical dimensions are different. Like DIN fittings, SMS fittings have a captured gasket and are tightened with a spanner wrench.

4. Bevel-seat fittings have precision-machined male and female portions that form a seal without a gasket. Like other threaded fittings, they can be easily rotated. In their external appearance, they are similar to John Perry fittings, because of the large hex nut used to tighten them. Bevel-seat fittings work very well when treated properly, but the metal-to-metal seal is easily damaged if abused. Bevel-seat fittings are occasionally used in breweries but are most commonly used in dairy processing plants.

18. How are cleanliness and sanitary efficacy measured?

One of the most effective means of judging the degree of cleanliness is visual inspection. The goal of cleaning is the removal of soil, and careful inspection after cleaning is a simple and powerful method. Flashlights are especially helpful when inspecting tanks and kegs. Knowing where to look is the key to effective visual inspection. Cleaning "shadows" around tank manways and temperature probes, sample lines on tanks, short deadlegs in pipe runs, areas hidden behind rubber gaskets, and the void under the false bottom of the lauter tun are a few places to look when inspecting equipment.

One method of assessing the effectiveness of cleaning uses riboflavin as a marker. A riboflavin solution is sprayed on the surface to be cleaned, the cleaning cycle is initiated (typically using only water), and the surface is inspected under ultraviolet light. Riboflavin glows when exposed to ultraviolet light, so that cleaning problems are easy to identify. This test is usually performed when equipment is being inspected prior to purchase. A tank cleaned with spray balls, for example, should show no signs of riboflavin.

19. Why should the pH of rinse water be measured?

While soil removal is the primary goal of cleaning, it is also important to completely rinse away the various chemical cleaners used in the brewery. Almost all cleaners fall into two categories: alkaline and acidic. Measuring the pH of the rinse water after cleaning helps to determine whether it contains chemical residue. The pH of the rinse water is high immediately following a caustic (sodium hydroxide) cleaning cycle and then drops as the rinsing cycle continues. It is important to know the initial pH of the water used for rinsing; most water from municipal supplies is slightly alkaline. Some brewers like to taste the rinse water after confirming the absence of chemical cleaners, to determine whether all flavors have been removed from the equipment being cleaned. Draft line cleaning is one task for which tasting is especially useful.

20. What microbiological methods are used to evaluate cleaning?

Historically, the success of the sanitizing step has been monitored with microbiological laboratory methods. Many methods and types of media are used, but all conventional methods involve the growth of microorganisms. When the goal is a sanitary environment, the desired outcome is negative test results. Although these methods are very reliable, they are also very time consuming and do not yield immediate results. Results typically follow days after the samples have been collected; hence, the brewer cannot immediately address a problem. This dilemma led to the development of rapid molecular biological techniques.

Rapid methods are designed to provide test results in hours, not days. Examples of rapid methods include ATP bioluminescence; the polymerase chain reaction (PCR), which relies on DNA amplification; and assays in which radioactive labels, such as O_{18} and H_3 (tritium), are used to monitor changes related to the growth of microorganisms. Many rapid methods never make it out of the development laboratory, because they are too expensive, are too difficult to perform, or utilize controlled testing reagents. ATP (adenosine triphosphate) bioluminescence is a rapid method that is fast and easy to perform and yields reliable data.

21. How does bioluminescence testing work?

The ATP bioluminescence test is a rapid and inexpensive method using an enzyme from fireflies (luciferase) and a substrate (luciferin). Luciferase catalyzes a change to luciferin when ATP is present. One of the byproducts of this reaction is light, and the amount of light emitted is related to the ATP concentration. The premise of this method is that any ATP present in a sample, typically on a swab, is associated with a bacterial population. False positives can occur, however, because ATP can be present after a bacterial population has been killed. The false positive potential can be minimized if a lysis step is included. This method is typically used as a go/no-go test.

22. What types of soils are typically found in breweries?

a. Protein soils are found in all areas of the brewery. Proteins are extracted from malt during mashing, and almost all the protein that coagulates upon heating precipitates as *teig* ("dough") and trub during mashing and lautering and especially during wort boiling. Cold-break trub forms when wort is cooled between the whirlpool and fermenter; cold-break soils are found in heat exchangers, wort lines, and fermenters. Stubborn protein-based soils formed by trub are found in hot-side brewhouse piping and equipment. Beer foam is rich in protein, and foam leaves protein soils after collapse. Foaming that occurs during fermentation, beer transfers, and batch carbonation in which a carbonating stone is used can lead to soil buildup.

b. Carbohydrate soils are found in all areas of the brewery and are easily removed by simple rinsing. However, when carbohydrates caramelize, crystallize, or are burned on, they are chemically changed into a soil that is much more difficult to remove. These soils are found in mash mixers, decoction kettles, and wort kettles.

The occurrence and intensity of carbohydrate soils can be minimized by equipment design. For example, if a steam jacket on a mashing vessel extends above the mash level, it can form a ring of concentrated wort that can caramelize and eventually become burned on. Wort kettles, especially stainless steel kettles, heated by direct flame or high-pressure steam (30 psig or more) foul more quickly than kettles heated with low-pressure steam (less than 30 psig). Copper brewhouse vessels, although no longer made by the major suppliers of brewing equipment, can be purchased on the used-equipment market. Copper has a higher heat transfer coefficient than stainless steel and also is more easily wetted, so that steam bubbles do not adhere to a copper surface as tightly as to stainless steel. These properties reduce wort burn-on in copper kettles, especially when high-pressure steam or direct flame is used as the heat source. Copper is still commonly used for internal heating coils.

c. Mineral deposits are common, especially where water or wort is heated. Hot-water tanks are frequently fouled with calcium carbonate, commonly referred to as lime. This mineral deposit forms when water containing calcium and carbonate or bicarbonate is heated. Lime deposits are extremely hard and form a tenacious ceramic-like film, which becomes increasingly difficult to remove as it increases in depth. Breweries located on limestone aquifers are most prone to this particular deposit.

Lime in utility water tanks can be minimized by using softened water. Calcium and magnesium are replaced by sodium in salt-based water softeners. Sodium bicarbonate deposits are associated with soft water, but this mineral deposit is much softer than calcium carbonate and is far easier to remove.

Calcium oxalate, $Ca_2(COO^-)_2$, or beer stone, forms on surfaces after prolonged contact with wort or beer. Beer stone has a brownish, translucent appearance and can be very difficult to remove if permitted to form a thick film. Oxalic acid, $C_2H_2O_4$ or $(COOH)_2$, is a common organic acid found in plants. Malt is the primary source of oxalic acid in the brewery.

d. Hop resins can form films on wort contact surfaces. This brewery-specific soil is especially prevalent in breweries producing highly hopped beers or using hop extracts. Hop resin films have a sticky texture, similar to that of pine tar. Routine cleaning with appropriate cleaners minimizes the accumulation of this soil.

e. *Brandhefe* (burnt yeast) is the combination of yeast and trub that forms "bathtub rings" and collects on ceilings in fermenters. Cold trub is commonly carried up into the kräusen during fermentation and deposits with yeast. *Brandhefe* has a firmer texture than yeast alone and is released in large pieces during rinsing and cleaning of fermenters.

f. Biological films caused by the growth of bacteria and fungi can form, especially equipment that sweats. Condensation, or sweating, occurs on cold surfaces occurs under humid conditions, and biological films typically form in such environments. Biological films can become thick and heavy and have a slimy appearance, and they are often dark brown or reddish. Fungal films that stain and can lead to degradation of certain materials, such as insulation, are commonly referred to as mildew. Examples are black "machine molds" on conveyors, stationary pumps, equipment, and piping.

g. Dust can be a problem in and around grain storage and milling areas. Malt dust contains bacteria, especially *Lactobacillus delbrueckii*, and acts as a vector transferring bacteria into wort and beer. Brewery workers can also transmit dust from grain-handling areas into sensitive areas of the brewery, such as the fermentation cellar. Proper housekeeping, including sweeping, vacuum cleaning, and dusting, should be regularly practiced in grain-handling areas.

Dust can cause explosions if it accumulates and a spark occurs. For this reason, many grain storage and milling rooms are equipped with devices (for example, louvered panels) that allow the rapid relief of gases that accompany an explosion.

Malt dust also irritates mucous membranes and can be bothersome to brewers who must work in a dusty environment. Prolonged exposure to malt dust can lead to allergies and infections.

23. How is a cleaning program developed?

The best approach in developing a cleaning plan is to first understand the nature of the soils present and the design of the equipment to be cleaned. Selection of the proper cleaning chemical depends upon the soil, and sometimes multiple cleaning steps with different chemicals are required. Understanding equipment design helps determine which parts can be cleaned in place and which parts require disassembly and manual cleaning. Some piping designs contain deadlegs, which cannot be adequately cleaned, and redesign may become a part of the cleaning strategy.

24. How are tanks cleaned?

Care must be exercised when a cold tank is cleaned with a hot cleaner and when a hot tank is rinsed with cold water. In both situations, a rapid change in pressure can occur, potentially leading to the collapse of the tank. Using a caustic cleaner in a tank filled with carbon dioxide poses the same problem with the creation of a vacuum, and it also results in a loss of chemical strength as the caustic reacts with the carbon dioxide. Two reactions can occur:

$$2NaOH + CO_2 \rightarrow Na_2CO_3 + H_2O \text{ (sodium carbonate) or}$$
$$NaOH + CO_2 \rightarrow NaHCO_3 \text{ (sodium bicarbonate).}$$

The sodium bicarbonate and/or sodium carbonate formed by these reactions will precipitate, and as a result a vacuum will be created, possibly strong enough to implode the tank. To prevent this problem, the side manways are commonly opened during cleaning. Some tanks do not have manways and must be equipped with pressure relief and vacuum relief valves of the proper size. However, tank vacuum safety valves are designed to keep a tank ventilated during pump-out, but they may not be able to protect the tank from sudden large changes in pressure during CIP and should not be relied upon for this task.

Caution: *Pressure relief valves and vacuum relief valves should be checked periodically to ensure that they are functioning properly.*

25. What properties make a cleaning compound an effective cleaner?

a. Wetting is the ability of a solution to penetrate soils and disperse the cleaning compounds of the detergent. Water and some cleaners, such as sodium hydroxide, have very high surface tension, which is associated with poor wetting. Surfactants ionize in solution to reduce surface tension and improve wetting. Surfactants tend to foam, which is why manual cleaning compounds are usually sudsy and are the best agents for soaking soiled fittings. Some wetting agents cause foaming problems; low-foaming wetting agents are typically selected for CIP applications where foaming is undesirable.

b. Organic-dissolving power is the ability of a chemical cleaner to chemically change and dissolve soils. It is very helpful to know the nature of the soil and to select a cleaner that is effective in dissolving the particular soil. Sodium hydroxide, for example, does not remove mineral deposits, and a brewer will quickly discover the futility of using the wrong cleaner when attempting to remove water deposits with caustic. However, caustic is very effective (and cost effective) in dissolving organic compounds, such as carbohydrates, resins, and peptonized proteins, into solutions that can be rinsed away.

c. Dispersion occurs when a cleaner helps to reduce the size of particles loosened from the surface of equipment and disperse them in solution. Silicates, phosphates, and surfactants are effective dispersants.

d. Protein removal requires chemicals that peptonize or reduce the size of protein molecules. Alkaline cleaners are very effective in dissolving peptonized proteins. Strong oxidants, such as chlorine and peroxide, are sometimes added to alkaline cleaners to break down and improve the removal of protein films.

e. Rinsibility is the relative ease of rinsing. Cleaners with poor rinsing properties require a larger volume of rinse water and present the risk of leaving residual cleaning solution on the surface being cleaned. Surfactants greatly improve rinsibility. However, surfactants that foam are as problematic as cleaners with poor rinsing properties, since some foams are difficult to collapse and drain from tanks.

f. Water-softening properties are important in the control of mineral scale buildup, especially calcium deposits. The most effective water-softening compounds act by binding (chelating) calcium. Water softening can also be facilitated by sequestrants, such as sodium tripolyphosphate, which form a water-soluble precipitant. Carbonates can be used to soften water, but the reaction produces calcium carbonate, which forms a scale on equipment.

g. Mineral-dissolving power is associated with acid cleaners and alkaline cleaners containing chelating agents, such as EDTA. Routine use of these types of cleaners can virtually eliminate the formation of mineral deposits on equipment surfaces.

26. What types of cleaning solutions are commonly used?

Alkaline cleaners are primarily used for the removal of heavy organic soils, such as trub from wort kettles, whirlpools, and wort coolers; yeast deposits from fermenters, serving vessels, transfer lines, beer hoses, and kegs; and protein deposits throughout the brewery.

Sodium hydroxide, commonly called caustic or caustic soda, is one of the most common alkaline cleaners. Sodium hydroxide has excellent organic-dissolving power (*Table 2.1*) and very good bactericidal properties, but it has poor wetting, dispersing, and rinsing properties. It also leads to the formation of calcium and magnesium sludge when mixed in hard water. Most caustics sold for brewery use are referred as built cleaners and contain other chemicals, such as surfactants and chelating agents, to make

Table 2.1. Relative action of common detergent constituents[a,b]

	Wetting	Organic-dissolving power	Dispersion	Protein removal	Rinsibility	Water softening	Mineral-dissolving power
Alkalies							
Sodium hydroxide	1	5	1	5	1	0	0
Sodium metasilicate	3	3	4	4	3	0	0
Sodium carbonate	1	2	1	2	1	0	0
Trisodium phosphate	2	2	4	4	3	0	0
Acids							
Organic acids	0	1–3	0	2	2	5	5
Mineral acids	0	1–4	0	0	0	5	5
Organics							
Sodium gluconate	0	0	0	0	0	5	3
EDTA	0	0	0	0	3	5	4
Surfactants	5	0	1	0	5	0	0

[a] Source: Barrett (1979).
[b] The higher the number, the greater the effect.

up for these deficiencies. Potassium hydroxide is sometimes used instead of sodium hydroxide, because it has better rinsing properties.

27. What are some concerns about alkaline detergents?

Sodium hydroxide and potassium hydroxide are strong bases and aggressively react with skin and mucous membranes. Great care must be exercised when caustic cleaners are used.

Brewers must always be aware that both sodium and potassium hydroxide react with carbon dioxide to form a solid carbonate deposit. A beer tank can quickly collapse when the CIP program is started if the tank to be cleaned is full of carbon dioxide gas. The reaction occurs very rapidly, and vacuum relief devices are of little help, because they are not designed to correct this problem. It is imperative to properly evacuate carbon dioxide from tanks prior to cleaning with caustic. Many brewers simply open the tank and wait for the heavy carbon dioxide to fall out. Some beer tanks are not equipped with manways located low on the tank, and fans must be used to bring air into these tanks prior to cleaning.

28. What alternatives to caustic cleaners can be used?

Sodium metasilicate is an effective cleaner and is safer to use and handle than caustic cleaners. It also has better wetting, penetration, and dispersing properties, but it has weaker organic-dissolving power.

Trisodium phosphate (TSP) is another alternative to caustic cleaners. It its cleaning properties, TSP is similar to sodium metasilicate.

TSP can be co-crystallized with sodium hypochlorite to form a cleaner known commercially as chlorinated TSP. This product can be used like chlorinated caustic or used as a chlorinated sanitizer.

Complex phosphates, such as sodium tripolyphosphate, are used primarily as detergent additives, because of their sequestering and dispersion properties. These compounds lose their sequestering ability at elevated temperatures and in a highly alkaline environment, and therefore they are typically not added to caustics and not used in CIP systems.

Restrictions were placed on the use of detergent phosphates in some areas of the United States in the 1970s, because of concerns about water pollution. Phosphates from detergents, fertilizers, and fecal waste can dramatically increase the growth of photosynthetic aquatic life, such as algae, and lead to a decrease in the dissolved oxygen content of water. Phosphates are now permitted in industrial cleaning formulations, but users of these chemicals should be aware of local environmental concerns about phosphate-containing effluents.

29. How does chlorine bleach affect cleaning?

Chlorine bleach (sodium hypochlorite) is frequently added to caustic cleaners specifically to help remove protein soils and hop resins. Chlorinated caustics are particularly effective for cleaning hot-side brewhouse equipment, including wort kettles, wort coolers, and transfer lines. The problem with chlorine is that it is corrosive to stainless steel, especially as pH decreases.

30. What problems can occur when bleach is added to a cleaning solution?

Chlorinated caustics can cause severe corrosion when the alkalinity of the cleaning solution decreases during use. Alkalinity is reduced in the normal course of cleaning, as the caustic reacts with the soils present.

Caution: *Caustic concentration must be maintained when bleach additives are used.*

A sudden decrease in alkalinity can occur when an alkaline cleaning cycle is followed by an acid cleaning cycle, if insufficient rinsing has been performed between cleaning cycles. Over time, this can result in rapid and severe pitting corrosion of equipment made with type 304 or type 316L stainless steel, the most common stainless steel alloys used in breweries.

31. Are there alternatives to bleach for cleaning protein soils?

Stabilized peroxides are an alternative to chlorine bleach. These compounds are a combination of peroxide and an organic carrier. Peroxides are very strong oxidizing agents and help remove protein films and hop resins in the same way that bleach does. Unlike bleach, peroxides do not corrode stainless steel. Because of the instability of these compounds, they are usually added to alkaline cleaners immediately before use or injected in-line in automated CIP systems.

32. How are acid detergents used?

Acid cleaners are routinely used for the removal of mineral deposits and beer stone throughout the brewery. Many brewers use acid cleaners exclusively in bright beer tanks, because these tanks are relatively easy to clean and acid cleaners do not react with carbon dioxide. This method reduces cleaning cycle time and carbon dioxide use.

33. How do acids compare in performance?

Phosphoric acid is the most widely used acid cleaner. (Like alkaline cleaners, acid cleaners contain additives to improve their wetting, rinsing, and dispersion properties.) Phosphoric acid works well as a mineral descaler, is not corrosive to stainless steel, and is safer to handle than strong acids.

Nitric acid is a strong, oxidizing acid and is blended with phosphoric acid to enhance cleaning strength and as a stainless steel conditioner. Concentrated nitric acid is dangerous to handle and emits noxious fumes, especially when heated. However, preformulated dilute acid cleaners containing nitric acid are commonly used. Nitric acid is effective in removing iron (rust) from the surface of stainless steel and helps to rebuild the passive layer (chromium oxide film) on stainless steel. Some brewers routinely passivate stainless steel equipment with a blend of nitric and phosphoric acids.

34. How do the materials from which equipment is made affect the selection of chemical cleaners?

Conventional equipment used in the brewing industry is typically made with type 304 or, less commonly, type 316L stainless steel. Stainless steel is durable, easy to maintain, and resistant to most chemicals used in breweries and food-processing plants. The most common cause of corrosion of stainless steel is chlorine, especially in acidic environments. Many companies avoid chlorine-related corrosion by simply not using chemicals that contain chlorine.

Aluminum was used in the past for certain brewing tools (e.g., yeast rakes and yeast sieves), beer kegs, and even fermenters. Caustics quickly corrode aluminum, and the result is very rapid dissolution of the material. Specially formulated caustics that are "aluminum inhibited" are available to alleviate this problem. Oxidizing acids, such as nitric acid, also attack aluminum. For these reasons, aluminum is no longer commonly used in the manufacture of brewing equipment and implements.

New equipment is rarely made from copper, with the exception of vessels clad in copper for decorative purposes, but this material was once widely used in the manufacture of brewhouse vessels. Copper is attacked by both alkaline and acid cleaners. Special cleaning formulations have been developed for use with copper and should be used in cleaning copper vessels or vessels containing copper components, such as heating coils and calandria parts.

35. How does detergent cleaning affect elastomers?

Elastomers used in gaskets, O-rings, and valve seats can be damaged by cleaners. One of the most common types of failures of elastomers is cracking. Cracks in elastomer seals result in leaks and harbor bacteria and soil. No elastomer is impervious to all conditions. Buna, EPDM, Viton, and silicone are among the most common and most resilient materials used for brewery applications.

36. How should new stainless steel brewing vessels be cleaned prior to use?

Stainless steel vessels typically arrive from the fabricator coated with cutting oils, grime, and dust, either from the fabrication process or picked up during shipping. Most tanks are covered in a protective plastic film, which leaves a residue when removed. These soils are normally removed with an alkaline cleaner having good grease-removal properties. One common degreaser is a sodium metasilicate cleaner with limonene (a citrus peel oil) added for improved grease cutting. The vessel interior is typically cleaned with a CIP device. The exterior is cleaned by rinsing with a hose, followed by manual cleaning with a nonabrasive scrubbing pad.

37. What is passivation?

New tanks typically receive some type of treatment to form a passive layer on the stainless steel surface prior to use. In the passive state, a molecular film of oxygen (frequently referred to as a chromium oxide film) covers the surface of the metal. The passive film forms spontaneously in environments containing molecular oxygen, when chromium atoms in the steel can react with oxygen. Thus stainless steel is normally passive. The surface layer gives stainless steel much of its resistance to corrosion.

38. How stable is a passivated surface?

Unlike passive films of other metals, the passive film of stainless steel is very stable. Also, it imparts protection to the metal even when molecular oxygen is no longer present in the environment, for example, in a tank full of beer. This stable passive film allows brewers to use stainless steel tanks to store beer for prolonged periods with little risk of corrosion.

39. What factors impede passivation?

Some soils and contaminants impede the formation of a passive film on a stainless steel surface. For example, on new equipment, machine oil, grease pencil marks, adhesives, organic deposits, and other soils can form an airtight film over stainless steel surfaces. Equipment surfaces may also be contaminated with iron from shop dust or road soils acquired during shipping, and iron can become embedded in stainless steel surfaces as a result of improper handling. Contamination with iron leads to rust. These soils and contaminants must be removed before the steel surface can fully passivate.

40. How is passivation accomplished?

Hot oxidizing acids are commonly used to remove iron contaminating the surface of stainless steel and to actively passivate the steel. The most frequently cited oxidizing acid solution used for passivation is nitric acid blended with phosphoric acid, applied at concentrations approaching 50% and at temperatures as high as 160°F (70°C). Hot mixtures of nitric and phosphoric acids are dangerous to handle and pose challenges for disposal, because of possible corrosion of sewer lines, and because of the nitrate component of the solution.

A safer alternative to nitric acid is citric acid. For passivation, a 0.6-molar solution of anhydrous citric acid (about 1 lb per gallon of deionized water), adjusted to pH 3.0–3.5 with ammonium hydroxide, is heated to

160°F (70°C) and recirculated through the CIP ball of the tank for about an hour. This solution can also be applied to problem areas with a brush or mop for a relatively safe spot treatment.

41. Are there situations in which additional treatment is needed?

Some stainless steel vessels contain embedded iron (e.g., iron from tools) that will cause corrosion if not removed. This type of contamination can be identified by rust that returns after repeated acid passivation. Grinding is a common and very effective method of removing embedded iron. Grinding should be done only by someone who is well qualified; an unskilled grinder can cause a lot of damage in a short time. Embedded iron can also be removed by pickling paste, a combination of nitric acid and hydrofluoric acid. It is recommended that pickling be performed by a qualified chemical cleaning contractor, since hydrofluoric acid is highly corrosive to flesh and bone, is toxic, and damages stainless steel if applied for too long.

42. How are tanks and equipment conditioned?

Aside from concerns about ferrous iron, many brewers are concerned about volatile constituents present in new elastomers used for valve seats, manway gaskets, and product hoses. Some brewers recirculate beer through the spray device of the tank in a closed loop for a specified time to "condition" the tank. The purpose is to dissolve beer-soluble compounds from elastomers that may be flavor active. The beer used for this process is discarded.

43. What are the key selection criteria for sanitizers?

A good brewery sanitizer should be

a. Nontoxic (like other sanitizers used in the food industry, brewery sanitizers must have no residual toxicity to humans)
b. Effective at killing a wide array of microorganisms
c. Fast-acting
d. Compatible with residual cleaning solutions
e. Noncorrosive to equipment

In addition, a good brewery sanitizer should not have the potential to negatively affect beer or beer flavor. However, even the best sanitizers can harm beer flavor or foam if used carelessly.

44. What types of sanitizers are commonly used?

a. Halogen-based sanitizers include sodium hypochlorite (bleach), iodine complexes (iodophors), and chlorine dioxide.

1. Bleach was discovered more than 200 years ago and was quickly applied in the textile industry. After Louis Pasteur discovered its disinfectant properties in the late nineteenth century, bleach became commonly used as a sanitizer. Sodium hypochlorite is a very effective sanitizer, but it has several limitations: it is unstable at high temperatures; reacts with soils and loses its sanitizing power; corrodes a wide array of metals, including stainless steel, under certain conditions; and reacts with phenolic compounds in beer to form chlorophenolic off-flavors.

2. Iodophors are a class of sanitizers composed of iodine bound to a large carrier molecule. The carrier is a surfactant, and iodophors quickly foam when pumped through an orifice, as in a spray ball. They also stain gaskets and hoses, and they lose potency over time, as a result of iodine release, especially when heated. In spite of these limitations, iodophors are very effective sanitizers, with broad-range activity at a relatively low concentration. They are not corrosive to stainless steel, are safe to handle, and can be used as no-rinse sanitizers in most areas. However, many brewers rinse out iodophors, to eliminate the possibility that an iodine aroma will carry over into the beer.

3. Chlorine dioxide is a nonfoaming, noncorrosive, and highly effective halogen-based sanitizer. The primary disadvantage of chlorine dioxide is that it is unstable, so it is typically generated on-site immediately before use. Generation systems are designed to react sodium chlorite with other chlorine compounds (sodium hypochlorite or hydrochloric acid) to produce chlorine dioxide, salt, and water ($5NaClO_2 + 4HCl \rightarrow 4ClO_2 + 5NaCl + 2H_2O$). Generation systems require trained operators and maintenance staff and an initial investment. Proprietary chemical blends liberate chlorine dioxide when activated with a weak acid, such as phosphoric acid, and do not require generators, but they still must be activated immediately prior to use.

b. Peroxyacetic acid (PAA) is a popular sanitizer made by binding acetic acid to hydrogen peroxide. PAA is a nonfoaming, noncorrosive, fast-acting sanitizer with broad-range activity over a wide temperature range. It decomposes into water, oxygen, and acetic acid, which are naturally present in beer, so that it adds nothing foreign to beer. Its most objectionable characteristics are its pungent aroma and rapid oxidizing action on skin and mucous membranes. Proper staff training and safety precautions should be implemented for the use of PAA, as for any other cleaning chemicals.

c. Heat is an excellent mode of sanitizing and sterilizing equipment and product. Life forms of all sorts can be eliminated by prolonged exposure to high temperature, although organisms differ in their response to heat treatment. Hot water, typically 180°F (80°C) or hotter, and steam are both commonly used in the food and beverage industries to sanitize and sterilize equipment. The most common application of hot-water sanitation in the brewery is in sanitizing heat exchangers, wort lines, filters, and kegs and in processing the product itself (for example, during wort boiling and pasteurization). A common process for heat sanitation of wort and beer lines is exposure to a temperature of 180°F (80°C) for 20 minutes. However, heat sanitation of brewing tanks is not a common practice, because it is impractical and uneconomical.

d. Quaternary ammonium compounds (quats or QACs) are a class of sanitizers composed of various organic alkyl compounds combined with the ammonium ion. Quats are surfactants and quickly foam, so they are unlikely candidates for CIP applications. Furthermore, they have a negative effect on beer foam and are typically not used on beer contact surfaces unless the surfaces are thoroughly rinsed. Ironically, quats are commonly used as glass sanitizers in some bars and restaurants in counties requiring that glassware be given a final rinse with an approved sanitizer. Quats are very effective, stable, biostatic compounds and are well suited for the prevention of mold growth and mildew formation on walls, floors, and the exteriors of cellar tanks and beer lines.

45. What type of equipment is available for brewery sanitation?

a. Manual cleaning. Manual cleaning implements, such as brushes, pads, cloths, and hand-held spray hoses, are the most basic tools used in sanitation. Tools selected for manual use must not scratch the surfaces being cleaned. Bristles should be soft, metal portions of tools should not touch equipment surfaces, scrub pads must not be abrasive, and cloths that are reused should be free of dirt and debris.

Some brewers make the mistake of cleaning stainless steel surfaces with scouring pads, such as Scotch-Brite pads used in kitchens. These abrasive pads increase the surface roughness of equipment and make subsequent removal of soils more difficult. Soft pads, such as sponges covered in an abrasive plastic material and pads similar to facial scrub pads, which do not scratch equipment, should be used instead.

Foamy detergents containing high amounts of wetting agents but of low alkalinity are normally used for manual scrubbing.

b. Spray devices.   Brewhouse vessels and cellar tanks are usually equipped with spraying devices for CIP. Spray devices commonly used in brewery vessels include spray dishes, static spray balls (***Figure 2.2***), rotating spray balls (***Figure 2.3***), and rotating cleaning machines (***Figure 2.4***).

Static spray dishes and spray balls are typically used in tanks where a combination of chemical strength, high temperature, and low mechanical action is effective for cleaning. Small tanks, bright beer tanks, and water tanks are examples of vessels in which these simple devices are used.

Rotating spray balls and cleaning machines are used in tanks of larger diameter and tanks with heavier soils, where greater mechanical force, or impingement, and the changing angle of spray facilitate cleaning. Brew kettles, fermenters, lagering tanks, and large bright beer tanks are examples of vessels typically cleaned with rotating spray devices. In these applications, higher impingement is used with lower temperatures and lower chemical strength.

Spray devices require liquid flow in order to function properly, and pump sizing is important. Performance curves are used to illustrate how changes in flow rate affect spray radius. A low flow rate produces a spray with a small radius. As the flow rate increases, the spray radius increases to a maximum, but if the flow rate is further increased the spray radius begins to fall off, because of atomization (misting). Impingement is also affected by flow and pressure. Flow velocity increases and pressure decreases when a flowing liquid is forced through a nozzle. Force is exerted when the liquid stream hits the surface being cleaned and rapidly decelerates (force = mass × acceleration).

46. What is turbulent flow?

Beer transfer lines and heat exchangers cannot be cleaned with spray devices. They are cleaned by the scrubbing action of turbulent liquid flow and the cleaning power of detergents. Turbulence in beer lines occurs at a velocity of 5–10 feet per second; excessive velocity leads to line erosion, noise, and the potential for severe water-hammer. The flow rates in ***Table 2.2*** correspond to 5 and 10 feet per second in lines of various sizes.

Figure 2.2. Low-impingement CIP spray ball. (Courtesy of Alfa Laval)

Figure 2.3. Moderate-impingement rotating CIP spray head. (Courtesy of Alfa Laval)

Figure 2.4. High-impingement rotating spray jet CIP machine. (Courtesy of Alfa Laval)

Table 2.2. Flow rates in tubes of various sizes

Outside diameter (in.)	Inside diameter (in.)	Flow rate (gallons per minute) at flow velocity of:	
		5 ft/s	10 ft/s
1.0	0.87	9	19
1.5	1.37	23	46
2.0	1.87	43	86
2.5	2.37	69	137
3.0	2.87	101	202

47. What is a simple way to clean a tank?

In the simplest form of a single-tank, single-use CIP system, the vessel being cleaned serves as the reservoir for the cleaning solution, and a portable pump is the only pump in the cleaning loop. This method is used in many small breweries, because it requires no additional investment in cleaning equipment beyond a spray device, which is included in the design of most tanks, and a portable pump, which is standard equipment for other brewery operations. This method also ensures that the hoses, fittings, and pumps are regularly cleaned.

48. What is a CIP system?

Multitank CIP systems designed for chemical recovery and reuse are common in large breweries that clean many tanks each day, where they quickly pay for themselves in chemical savings, reduced cleaning labor, reduced water use, and reduced preparation time. *Figure 2.5* is a piping and instrumentation diagram of a typical three-tank CIP system, equipped with the following features:

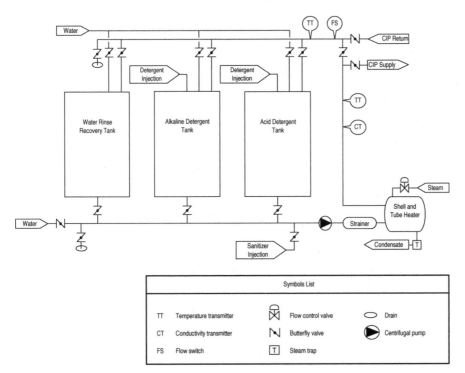

Figure 2.5. Piping and instrumentation diagram of a typical three-tank CIP system.

   a. Chemical dosing pumps for alkaline cleaner, acid cleaner, and sanitizer
   b. In-line steam heat exchanger to heat the cleaning solution
   c. Temperature sensors
   d. Conductivity sensors for monitoring chemical strength
   e. Flow sensors for "proof-of-flow" in the return line
   f. Level measurement in tanks for monitoring the tank level and automatic addition of makeup water

These features improve the consistency of cleaning by removing some of the common sources of human error in cleaning. Most CIP systems are automatically controlled by programmable logic controllers (PLCs) and operated through an operator interface. Many CIP control systems are equipped with data-logging equipment to record and print key information, such as cleaning temperature, chemical strength, and solution flow rate. Such reports can play an important part in a cleaning quality assurance program.

Most breweries with chemical reuse CIP systems have dedicated systems for different areas of the brewery, to prevent cross-contamination of soils. For example, the same CIP system usually is not used for cleaning both the brewhouse and the cellar tank.

49. What is a typical CIP cycle?

All CIP systems, whether simple or complex in design, are used in a similar fashion. A typical CIP cycle consists of the following steps:

   a. Prerinse
   b. Chemical wash
   c. Rinse
   d. Sanitization
   e. Final rinse

Variations on the basic sequence include multiple chemical wash and rinse steps (usually an alkaline wash followed by an acid wash) and processes combining sanitization and final rinse in a single step. Typical cleaning sequences for brewhouse vessels, fermenters, bright beer tanks, and transfer lines are shown in *Table 2.3*. Cleaning times and temperatures vary depending on the chemicals used, the chemical strength, and soil loading. Rinsing times also vary, depending on the soil load, the rinsing properties of the cleaner, and the method of rinsing (burst rinsing or continuous rinsing).

Table 2.3. Typical cleaning-in-place (CIP) cycles in the brewery

Equipment (soil type)	CIP step	Temperature	Time (min.)
Brewhouse vessels[a] (protein, beer stone)	Water prerinse	Ambient	2–5
	Alkaline/oxidizer wash	120–160°F (50–70°C)	30–60
	Water postrinse	Ambient	5–10
	Acid wash (periodic)	Ambient	20–40
	Water final rinse	Ambient	5–10
Fermenters (yeast, protein, mild beer stone)	Water prerinse	Tempered	5–10
	Alkaline wash	80–140°F (25–60°C)[b]	45–60
	Water postrinse	Tempered	5–10
	Acid wash (periodic)	Ambient	20–40
	Water postrinse	Ambient	5–10
	Sanitization, final rinse	Ambient	15–30
Bright beer tanks (beer, foam, mild beer stone)	Water prerinse	Ambient	2–5
	Acid wash	Ambient	30–60
	Water postrinse	Ambient	5–10
	Alkaline wash (periodic)	Ambient	30–60
	Water postrinse	Ambient	5–10
	Sanitization, final rinse	Ambient	15–30
Transfer lines (wort, protein, yeast, beer stone)	Water prerinse	Ambient	5–10
	Alkaline wash	120–160°F (50–70°C)	45–60
	Water postrinse	120–160°F (50–70°C)	5–10
	Acid wash (periodic)	120–160°F (50–70°C)	20–40
	Water postrinse	Ambient	5–10
	Sanitization, final rinse	Ambient	15–30

[a] Frequency of cleaning and chemical selection varies for brewhouse vessels. For example, brew kettles are cleaned more frequently and intensely than mash mixers.
[b] A hot cleaning cycle in a fermenter should be preceded and followed by tempered water rinse cycles, to minimize the magnitude of temperature and pressure changes.

50. What is burst rinsing?

Burst rinsing is a method of rinsing in bursts lasting from a few seconds to a few minutes but allowing complete drainage of the tank between cycles. This method is more effective than continuous rinsing, because it shortens the duration of the rinsing step and reduces water consumption.

Summary

The subject of brewery sanitation may not be as exciting as topics directly pertaining to beer and brewing, but sanitation is part and parcel of what we do as brewers. A solid understanding of sanitation coupled with rigorous application of its principles is guaranteed to generate tangible benefits. A good sanitation program extends equipment life and improves overall performance. Public perception is based largely on appearance, and a clean, tidy brewery is perceived much more favorably than a dirty, disorganized plant. Finally, a good sanitation program improves the quality and consistency of the product by combating contamination that affects beer quality.

REFERENCES

Anonymous. 2002. Partners in grime. *The Brewer International* 2(8):30–32.

Barrett, M. 1979. Detergents and sterilants in the brewery. The Cass Lectures, Spring 1979.

Boulton, C., and Quain, D. 2001. *Brewing Yeast and Fermentation.* Blackwell Scientific, Oxford.

Lewis, A. S. 2001. Stress corrosion. *The New Brewer,* July–August, pp. 37–45.

Marriott, N. G. 1985. *Principles of Food Sanitation.* Van Nostrand Reinhold, New York.

O'Rourke, T. 2003. CIP—Cleaning in place. *The Brewer International* 3(4):30–34.

CHAPTER 3

Draft Dispense

Jaime Jurado
The Gambrinus Company

1. Why is draft technical training important?

Draft beer is a perishable product with specific parameters such as carbonation level and clarity. Even with excellent refrigeration, draft beer deteriorates over time. To assure that customers experience beer as intended by the brewer, professional technical management of draft dispense is required. Comprehensive knowledge of the fundamentals of draft engineering, terminology, hardware standards, and appropriate cleaning protocols is essential for any professional draft technician.

2. What knowledge is required by draft technicians?

The expertise sufficient to troubleshoot dispense problems, to properly clean and maintain dispense equipment, to evaluate beer-clean glassware, and to provide hands-on assistance is the benchmark of the draft dispense professional.

3. Where can a brewer or retailer find draft training?

In North America, the Draught Beer Guild (www.draughtbeerguild.com) is a good start. Private courses on draft skills are available from the Siebel Institute. Dispense equipment companies also offer courses, and professional draft technician training is provided by breweries.

Table 3.1. Dimensions of standard U.S. Sankey and Hoff-Stevens kegs (in inches)

Keg type	Diameter	Height	Height with coupler
Half-barrel U.S. Sankey	16½	23½	29
Quarter-barrel U.S. Sankey	16½	13½	19
Slim quarter-barrel	11.15	23¼	29
U.S. 5-gal "pony 1/6-bbl"	10	24½	30
Hoff-Stevens	17¼	22½	29

4. What are the dimensions of Hoff-Stevens and Sankey straight-wall (U.S.) kegs?

The dimensions of typical Sankey and Hoff-Stevens kegs are given in *Table 3.1*.

Careful use of kegs of various sizes allows a retailer to maximize the variety of beers drawn from a space-limited cold box. In the space needed to accommodate two 1/2-barrel Sankey straight-wall kegs, one can readily place the same two kegs as well as two 1/6-barrel kegs or the same two kegs and one slim 1/4-barrel keg. A three-keg box (designed for three 1/2-barrel kegs) can fit the three kegs plus two slim 1/4-barrel kegs.

5. What keg connectors are used in North America?

The most common keg coupler in North America is the Sankey standard. There are North American and European versions, which are similar but not interchangeable.

There is also a "two-probe" standard, the Hoff-Stevens keg coupler, which consists of two tube-shaped spears with a figure-8-shaped rubber seal wrapped around them. However, the use of Hoff-Stevens kegs is declining every year, because these kegs have no hand holes, are larger in diameter than the Sankey kegs, and cannot be washed and filled automatically.

Imported beers feature European Sankey, Grundy Tri-Lobe, German A (slider), and other types that require unique couplers. At least one brewery offers kegs with a connector specific for its brands.

6. What is the highest pressure one might apply to a keg with the applied gas?

In a Hoff-Stevens keg, pressure should never exceed 40 pounds per square inch (psig), and in a Sankey straight-wall keg, the pressure should not exceed 55 psig.

Table 3.2. Kegs poured in relation to CO_2 cylinder size

Cylinder size (lb)	Kegs poured
2.5	5
10	10
20	40

7. How much CO_2 is needed to dispense a 15.5-gallon (U.S.) keg of beer?

Approximately 5/8 of a pound of CO_2 is required in a leak-free system (*Table 3.2*).

8. What is "internal pressure" in a keg?

The internal pressure of a keg is the gauge pressure that exists naturally in the sealed, untapped keg. CO_2 pressure is a natural component of every beer keg. Carbonated beer contains dissolved gas, and the internal pressure of a keg is dependent on the temperature of the beer in the keg and its carbonation level.

9. Is there a significance to knowing the internal pressure?

The internal pressure represents a starting point in dispense design, because proper dispense requires that pressure applied to a keg be approximately 3 psig above its internal pressure. If the applied pressure is lower than the internal pressure, the beer goes flat over time; if the applied pressure is approximately 4 psig or more above the internal pressure, the beer in the keg overcarbonates over time. Internal pressure is the inherent pressure of pure CO_2 gas inside the headspace of a keg that maintains set-point carbonation. It is dependent on the beer temperature, which in turn is dependent on the cold room temperature.

10. What factors dictate beer dispense driven from a CO_2 cylinder?

The applied pressure necessary to properly dispense beer varies among installations. If the dispense pressure on the keg is 5 or 6 psig above the internal pressure, some of the dispense gas diffuses and is absorbed by the beer, resulting in overcarbonation and foamy beer at the faucet. If the dispense gas pressure is less than the internal pressure, undercarbonation occurs and the beer goes flat.

11. How can a brewer and a retailer easily assess the effectiveness of their line cleaning?

A brewer can conduct a rapid hygiene test using a luminometer, which amplifies adenosine triphosphate (ATP) residuals. Bar staff can visually inspect the draft dispense system and look carefully for biofilm buildups, molds, and slime. After a keg coupler is disconnected, a visual inspection of that coupler is important. Once disconnected, the faucet can be removed with a standard spanning wrench and disassembled and the internal surface of the shank inspected. A simple test for deposits is to roll up a paper napkin and wipe the inner surface of the tube inside the shank. It should not have any deposits.

The easiest test is to taste the beer before the line has been cleaned and then taste again after cleaning. It should taste the same, or better, after the line clean.

12. Is there an appropriate methodology for use of a luminometer?

Before the line clean is initiated, several distinct points in the system are carefully swabbed. The swabs are tested for ATP residue with the luminometer, and the output is recorded. The process is repeated immediately after cleaning. A 1-log reduction in output in relative light units (RLU) generally indicates that the cleaning is adequate. Several sample points in a test are required because luminometers are inherently "noisy" instruments. It is possible to find that the RLU output of a particular sample point is much higher after cleaning than before, but by taking samples at several points, these outliers can be removed from the data.

13. What concerns exist in draft systems from a microbiological perspective?

Lactic acid bacteria, acetic acid bacteria, pediococci (bacteria in the genus *Pediococcus*), bacteria in the family Enterobacteriaceae and the genera *Zymomonas* and *Pectinatus,* brewery yeast, and beer-spoilage wild yeasts are some of the microbiological threats to draft beer dispense. If regular cleaning is inadequate, infections by these microorganisms may be manifested in off-taste, haze, ropiness, mustiness, acidity, and other defects.

14. How frequently should draft dispense lines and systems be cleaned?

Cleaning the entire system every two weeks, from keg coupler to faucet and everything in between, is considered an acceptable standard by most North American brewers. Elsewhere, such as in Great Britain, the standard is once a week.

In the United States, the standard may vary according to state and municipal laws, and it is important to clean at the frequency specified by local laws. For example, under the Connecticut Liquor Control Board Law S 30-6-A23, draft beer dispense systems must be cleaned every 7 days. In an adjacent state, the Massachusetts Alcoholic Beverage Control Commission Law 3 2.05 CMR specifies that draft dispense systems must be cleaned twice per week.

15. What line cleaning chemicals should be used?

a. Alkaline detergents are based on sodium hydroxide at 2–3% concentration (by weight).

A product formulated with surfactants and wetting agents is generally effective. Alternative formulations that contain potassium hydroxide also work, as do formulations that combine both caustic agents. There are also alkaline detergents available that do not contain either of these common bases.

b. Acidic detergents are also available for periodic use to remove accumulated beer stone from draft dispense hardware. Most of them contain solutions of phosphoric acid.

The most important point is to use a product that is "brewery-approved" at the manufacturer's recommended concentration. Powdered cleaners with "no-rinse" formulations are available, but they are problematic because they leave a visible film. Although the film consists of a coating that helps prevent the active ingredient from caking and not the active ingredient itself, in a brewery, no one would leave detergent residue in a line and then flush it out with beer, and neither should someone in the field.

16. How does one clean a beer line?

There are three approaches, all including a common element: the faucets and keg couplers are carefully and thoroughly manually scrubbed. Before the keg couplers are reconnected at the end of the clean, the keg valves are carefully flushed of beer and wiped with clean paper towels or tipped to remove rinse water.

a. Line soak.   In the most common process, the line is cleaned in the direction of the beer flow through the system. The beer keg is disconnected, and the keg coupler is connected to a canister of water or a water flush connector. All beer is moved out, and the line is thoroughly "pushed out" with water. Next, a canister of detergent at appropriate strength is attached and drawn through the line, and a static soak of 15–20 minutes is allowed. (Note: One international brewery offers its own branded beer line cleaner and specifies a 60-minute line soak). Finally, clean rinse water is pushed through the line to remove the detergent solution, and then the line is either blown out with beer gas or reconnected to the keg and the water drawn out until the beer-water interface is clearly dumped through the faucet.

A line length of 40 ft is generally the maximum that can be cleaned well by a line soak. However, if the interval between cleanings does not exceed 2 to 3 weeks, the soak method has been demonstrated to be an effective means of cleaning in longer installations.

b. Line circulation.   A superior approach is similar to the brewery clean-in-place (CIP) procedure. A recirculation loop is built that captures all keg couplers and incorporates every beer dispense line. Clean water initially clears beer from the loop and is run to a drain, and then a detergent solution is recirculated through the loop for a period of 10–20 minutes. (Note: A warm solution maximizes efficacy). Upon completion of this step, the loop is emptied to a drain, and clean, cold water is pumped through the loop to remove detergent. The loop is finally "blown through" by dispense gas or reconnected to the beer kegs so that beer can be drawn through the lines to displace the water. Beer line cleaning pumps driven by 1/10- to 1/4-horsepower motors are effective. The larger pumps provide higher velocities, which maximize turbulent flow and surface shear near the beer tube wall. However, the larger the pump or motor, the greater the need for an adjustable bypass from outlet to inlet to throttle the pump for shorter loops.

c. Cleaning sponges.   Incorporation of cleaning sponges in the cleaning cycle is an established and proven best practice, but sponges in the line clean do not work when there are hardware items such as flow-of-beer stop detectors and pumps in the dispense system. Bypasses must be arranged to adapt such installations for sponges. The sponges can be introduced manually into the beer dispense loop, but one can also purchase

Figure 3.1. Top, a sponge (shown by arrow) traveling through the cleaning loop. Bottom, an installation designed for sponge cleaning. Any such system must be free of components that might trap sponges.

convenient units, and at least one German vendor represented in North America offers recirculating pump options with integral sponge-ball insertion in a convenient package. *Figure 3.1* shows an installation designed for sponge cleaning.

A concern with pump systems is overpressurization of the loop, which can cause disconnections at weak couples, fittings, or clamps. Most U.S. pumps have a maximum pressure of 40 psig, but some have a variable return from the pump outlet to the inlet, the bypass valve, that must be manually closed or opened partially to tune the pump pressure outlet. These pumps should be initialized with the bypass valve fully open at start and then adjusted to achieve good circulation. Some manufacturers incorporate a pressure output gauge in the pump, an excellent feature.

17. What is the optimum temperature for line cleaning?

Manufacturers and vendors often do not comment on temperature of use, but it is known that a 10° increase in temperature effects a doubling of the cleaning efficacy for a given detergent solution. Because a dispense system is made up of various components connected to each other, a pragmatic maximum cleaning temperature is 125°F (52°C). In python systems, the glycol system should be stopped (or at least recirculation through the python is stopped) during the clean to prevent the detergent solution from cooling down excessively. It is optimal to use a cold rinse solution, and including ice in the water is good, so that the lines can be cooled and packed with ice water before beer is drawn through them again after the clean.

18. How does one clean a stained line?

After the line has been soaked in detergent solution, a long, flexible brush can be used. There are brushes specially made to scour beer tubes, or a trombone cleaner (sold in music stores) can also be used. The trombone cleaner is flexible and has a reach of 4 ft, so one can clean 4 ft at each end of the tube, and each side has a different-sized brush.

For long lines, adding sponges to the recirculating pumped detergent solution can help remove the protein film.

Chlorine bleach products should never be used because of taint problems and chlorophenol concerns. A nonchlorine oxidizer is helpful in cleaning a stained line.

19. What is the technique for cleaning beer faucets?

The faucet is disassembled and rinsed in water, and then all surfaces and the two vent holes are carefully brushed. Pipe cleaners can also be used to clean the vent holes. For optimal cleaning, the components are rinsed and brushed again with a draft dispense detergent and then rinsed a final time with clear water before reassembly. The design of the standard faucet requires regular cleaning to maintain its hygienic state.

Some faucets are sold that are described by the vendors as "clean through" faucets, but these require periodic disassembly and inspection, at the very least. There are also alternatives to the standard North American faucet that offer vent-free design and superior cleanability. A vent-free faucet and a typical North American faucet are shown in *Figure 3.2*. The faucet on the right remains mostly flooded internally with beer, which eliminates the aerobic environment concerns (beer within stays

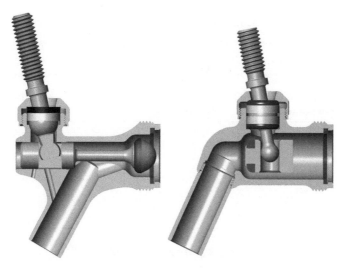

Figure 3.2. A standard North American faucet (left) and a vent-less faucet (right). (Courtesy of Ventmatic Company, Inc. Reprinted, by permission, from Jurado, 2003a)

cool due to conduction from the faucet walls). The standard faucet on the left seals at the back, and the faucet drains, leaving a wetted beer surface with aerobic exposure.

20. What options exist for beer lines?

The brewer naturally favors stainless steel tubing, but installation costs normally preclude its use. Stainless tubing is listed by outside diameter (OD), while vinyl and polymer tubing are listed by inside diameter (ID). Thus, a 5/16-in. stainless tube fits inside a 5/16-in. vinyl tube!

The use of barrier tube trunk lines in draft dispense has been established as a best practice. Barrier tubing has an inner lining of nylon 11 or modified polyethylene terephthalate (PET) and offers several functional advantages over vinyl, linear low-density polyethylene (LLDPE), and polymer tubing: the smoother surface means less resistance to beer flow through the tube (lower friction factor), and the barrier lining protects the beer tube from flavor taints from products. It also essentially stops the diffusion of oxygen and the escape of CO_2 from the beer through the tube wall. Barrier tubing is not as flexible as polyvinyl tubing, so for connections to keg couplers, clear polyvinyl tubing is used most often. To increase restriction in a set-up, loops of small-bore, low-linear density polyethylene are convenient. They are often kept tightly coiled and installed as near the faucet as is practical.

Table 3.3. Temperature changes in a half-barrel keg in two environments

Time required to chill a half-barrel keg of beer to 38°F in a cooler set at 36°F		Temperature increase of beer in a half-barrel keg in still air at 79°F, from a starting temperature of 38°F	
Initial temperature (°F)	Hours	Hours	Initial temperature (°F)
50	25	0	38
48	23.5	1	39
46	21	2	41
44	18	3	42
42	13.5	4	43
40	7	5	45
38	0	6	48

21. How long does a keg take to warm or cool?

Kegs must be kept refrigerated at all times, until empty. The warming and cooling rates are dependent on the temperature of the environment in which the kegs are placed.

The cooling and warming rates of a keg in two different temperature environments are given in *Table 3.3.*

22. What temperature is ideal for a cold box?

Temperatures of 35–38°F (2–3°C) are ideal for many beers, but cask-conditioned ales may need to be kept warmer, according to the recommendation of the brewery. It is possible to make a warm zone in an otherwise cold box. Such a strategy is useful for serving cask-conditioned ales as well as cold lagers from the same box.

Brewers should specify the temperature of storage and delivery, because there are differences. A respected German brewer insists on dispensing highly carbonated hefeweizen at 50°F (10°C). Many American brewers specify a range not to exceed 41°F (5°C) for dispense temperature to inhibit the growth of microbes.

When requirements for a cold box installation are specified, realistic inclusion of compensation for traffic in the box, drainage, the number of kegs to be delivered per week, and heat gain from the outside ambient temperature must be considered in order to properly determine the refrigeration load.

23. At what temperatures should lagers and ales be poured?

The dispense temperature range should be specified by the brewery. Lagers and ales are generally served colder in North America than in

Table 3.4. Suggested dispense temperatures[a]

	°C	°F
Very cold lagers	5–7	40–44
Lagers	7–9	44–48
Keg ales	8–10	45–50
Cask ales	11–13	52–56

[a] Data courtesy of I. Swanson, Young's and Co.'s Brewery, London.

Europe, and in Europe one finds guidelines in the literature. *Table 3.4* shows suggested draft beer serving temperatures.

24. How are beer lines specified in draft dispense installations?

Typically, the inside diameter (ID) of the beer line is specified.

a. Gas line is generally 5/16-in. ID and of braided material if the pressure is greater than 40 psig.

b. Jumper lines, the flexible lines attached to the keg couplers, are mostly 3/8-in. ID polyvinyl.

c. Trunk line, the long tubing that carries beer from the more flexible jumper line to the choker line, ranges from 1/4-, 5/16-, or 3/8-in. ID. This material can be polyvinyl, but semirigid barrier hose is recommended. The larger ID reduces line friction (discussed later).

d. Choker line, used to help balance the system flow at the font, is often 3/16-in. ID polyvinyl or linear low density polyethylene (LLDPE).

Because of hygienic requirements, materials approved by the U.S. Food and Drug Administration (FDA) must be specified.

25. How is forced-air cooling implemented?

A forced-air system requires air ducting, a blower of appropriate size, and a closed-loop system for delivering cold air to the dispense point and then sending it back to the walk-in cooler. *Figure 3.3* illustrates typical features. Note that the design must account for total cold air duct/conduit length.

26. How far from the cold box can forced-air cooling be used?

A forced-air system sends cold air from a cold box over some distance and returns warm air to the box. For the distance traveled, beer trunk lines run inside the cold-air conduit to keep them cold. This is a relatively

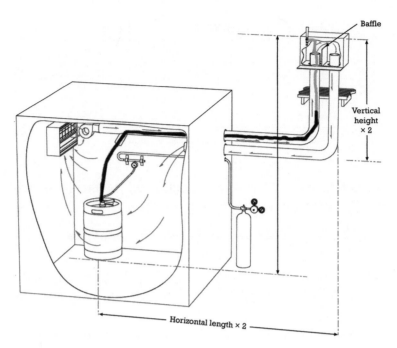

Figure 3.3. Forced-air system implementation. (Reprinted, by permission, from Jurado, 2003c)

inexpensive method of chilling beer lines and font, generally provided that the line run is less than 30 ft. Warm air is returned to the cold box, either through a separate return conduit or more often through an insulated pipe that includes the cold air from the cooler and the beer lines (*Figure 3.4*). The air is driven down a duct by a fan (e.g., with a capacity of 75 standard cubic feet per minute). The practical limits depend on the cooling capacity of the cold box to recool returned air from the system and the ability of the blower fan to keep the duct cool enough. Installations of up to 35 ft have been successful, but a forced-air system is much simpler for straight installations and a distance outside the box of 10 ft. If the walk-in cooler is suitably specified for chilling capacity, longer runs of ductwork can be supported by forced-air cooling; however, the glycol bundle (python) system (discussed later) is more often used for cooling beer lines when the distance from the walk-in exceeds 30 ft.

27. What are the important parameters of a forced-air system design?

The use of forced air to keep beer lines cool from the cold box to the faucet requires a cooling system in the keg box that has adequate capacity

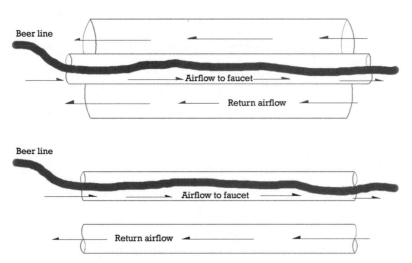

Figure 3.4. Options for forced-air delivery and return systems: a loop (bottom) and the more efficient tube-in-tube-installation (top). (Reprinted, by permission, from Jurado, 2003b)

to maintain all kegs at the target temperature and also cool the closed air loop for the dispense.

In *Figure 3.4* (top), the shaft installation uses an inner tube of 3-in. diameter and an outer tube of 4-in. diameter. The beer lines and the fresh cold air supply are within the inner tube, and air is returned via the outer line.

In *Figure 3.4* (bottom), a shaft carries the beer lines and contains two flexible or rigid polyvinyl chloride (PVC) tubes of 2- to 3-in. diameter, which are taped together and insulated. The line containing the beer tubes is also supplied with air from the cold box by a centrifugal blower. The second tube is for the return of cold air to the keg box. If the outer tube is well insulated, this is an energy-efficient system.

The shank and beer faucet are enclosed in an airtight channel or box. Cold air from the cooler circulates within the box or channel and then is sent back to the keg box continuously.

Note: Each 90-degree bend is equivalent to 5 ft of length.

28. What is the correct duct size for a forced-air installation?

A duct with a 2-in. ID is appropriate for two beer lines, and 4-in. ID is needed for eight beer lines. Insulation at least 1/2 in. thick is recommended to minimize heat gain in the cold recirculating air.

29. **What blower size should be specified?**

Determination of the correct blower is based on several factors: whether a single-header flexible duct is used with a 3-in. ID beer line duct and a 4-in. ID return air duct, whether a beer line duct and a return duct of the same size (2-, 3-, or 4-in. ID) are used, or whether rigid air ducts made of PVC are used. An additional factor is the number of beer lines specified to run in the beer line duct. As guidelines, with up to four beer lines to cool, these figures represent conservative starting points:

> 15 cubic feet per minute (cfm) for direct-draw boxes that cool only the font tower immediately above the box
>
> 60 cfm for runs not longer than 8 ft (16 ft of duct overall)
>
> 140 cfm for 3-in. flexible or rigid tubing not longer than 20 ft (40 ft of duct overall)
>
> 265 cfm for 3- or 4-in. flexible or rigid tubing not longer than 30 ft (60 ft of duct overall)

30. **When is a glycol-cooled bundled system ("python") appropriate?**

Use of glycol systems for cooling beer lines longer than 30 ft is typical. A "python" is the industry-standard designation for an insulated beer line bundle that also includes coolant line supply and return. Pythons can contain just a few beer lines or can be large and contain a number of beer lines and several coolant line supplies and returns.

Long draw runs are ideal for python implementation. The objective is to prevent or minimize heat transfer to the beer, thereby keeping the beer temperature at the faucet as close to the keg temperature as possible. Tight insulation to prevent loss of cold air minimizes the load on the cold box. Distances of 150 ft can be accommodated routinely with glycol python systems.

Glycol python installations are commonly referred to as *closed remote systems.*

31. **How does one specify a python in a draft dispense application?**

Manufacturers of python bundles can best recommend the optimal bundle for a specific installation. Outer insulation thickness varies and might depend on the parameters of the specific installation. Many installations are served well with 1/2-in.-thick open cell insulation.

Figure 3.5. Python bundle consisting of a sealed PVC outer protective layer, open-cell flexible foam insulation protected from moisture by a vapor barrier wrap (moisture strapping), and the beer line bundle surrounded by an aluminum wrapping to provide even cooling along the outer contact points of the beer lines. (Reprinted, by permission, from Jurado, 2003b)

The second part of the specification is the cooling medium (chilled water or propylene glycol solutions), which runs through the coolant feed lines in the python and returns in the return lines, often circulating through the font to keep the beer faucets cold.

Finally, because pythons are prefabricated and come in a variety of configurations to accommodate different numbers of beer lines, many retailers specify pythons with an extra line that may not be used at the time the python is commissioned but is available for future use. Pythons are convenient because beer dispense lines have a finite lifetime and then must be replaced. In most cases, the lifetime does not exceed 10 years. Replacing lines at the frequency recommended by the manufacturer is the best practice.

Quality python systems incorporate vapor barriers and an external shroud over the insulation (*Figure 3.5*).

32. How far from the cold box can glycol cooling be used?

A standard glycol recirculation system contains a sealed refrigerant, and maintaining suction at 20–21 psig (in a typical midrange chiller) achieves a glycol temperature of 34°F (1°C) for the standard 50% water–50% glycol chilling medium. Glycol powerpacks are specified in several ways, for example, by horsepower and heat rejection load in BTUs (British thermal units). For a very long installation, such as in a sports arena or casino, additional near-end final chillers are available and can easily be plumbed in. Glycol powerpack systems come in many sizes and can easily keep cold a well-made python bundle of beer lines with coolant line (and coolant return line) wrapped in proper insulation and a vapor and moisture barrier.

The target glycol temperature is generally verified and adjusted (if needed) at installation. Generally, the longer the python, the colder the glycol needs to be.

Very long runs of beer lines from the walk-in cooler are possible with a well-specified glycol system and a well-installed python system.

33. What are some rules of thumb for glycol powerpack implementation?

A 1/3-HP compressor is generally adequate for four beer lines up to 75–100 ft long. A 1/2-HP compressor is adequate for distances up to 250 ft, and a 3/4-HP is appropriate for 350 ft.

Avoidance of hot spots in the line route is critical. Longer runs can require lower coolant temperatures. A safe minimum temperature for glycol is 28°F (–2°C).

34. How is glycol cooling implemented in a python system?

Figure 3.6 illustrates a standard powerpack installation with flow-of-beer stop detectors (FOBs) and individual secondary regulators for each keg. The glycol line connects to the python inside the cooler, and the glycol return line separates from the python inside the cooler, to ensure that there are no warm spots in the lines leaving the cold box. Because of the inclusion of a coolant loop, the manufactured python bundle must include protection against accumulation of moisture from condensation, and good pythons are engineered with such protection.

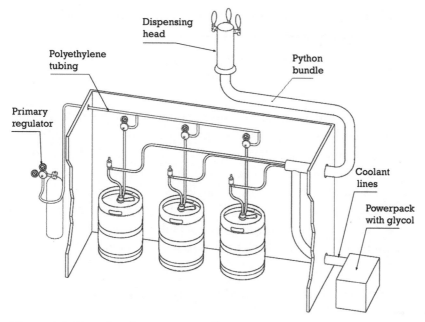

Figure 3.6. Typical python system installation.

35. What common problems arise in glycol installations?

One problem with glycol systems in warm, humid environments is that continual condensation is possible. If the reservoir is not sealed completely, and many are not, condensation of moisture in the solution causes dilution, resulting in an ice buildup on the reservoir cooling surface (typically on the coils). The accumulated ice insulates the cooling surface, and the reservoir warms.

Dirt fouls the heat dissipation fins of glycol powerpacks, so a coil cleaner must be sprayed on periodically to clean the surfaces. The same type of cleaner is useful for cleaning blower-evaporators in walk-in coolers.

36. What is the ideal time for tapping a keg once it has been delivered to the cold box?

Twenty-four hours to allow the keg to settle and approach target temperature is ideal. A distribution system may have been set up so that keg delivery trucks are loaded hours before deliveries commence, and if the kegs are not kept at the temperature of the keg vault at the distributorship, the warming beer, agitated inside the kegs by the normal bumps in the road, creates challenges if the kegs are tapped soon after delivery.

37. What concerns exist with the use of serving tanks instead of kegs?

The four Cs guide the use of serving tanks:

a. Capacity.   The tanks should be of an appropriate size, so that no tank holds beer longer than an agreed time, such as 10 days.

b. Cleanability.   Careful attention should be given to the cleanability of both the serving tanks and the dispense end.

c. Cooling.   It is critical to cool the beer in the tank to a specified temperature, and keeping beer at the target temperature between the tank outlet and the faucet is often a challenge.

d. Carbon dioxide.   The level of CO_2 must be maintained throughout the volume of beer remaining in the tank once it has been tapped, so attention to proper balancing of the system with applied CO_2 pressure is important.

38. Why can't pure carbon dioxide be used for dispensing any beer from any installation?

CO_2 is a fine dispense medium, but options are needed for long-draw systems. The gas pressure delivered to a keg in order to dispense the beer normally must be increased as the distance from the faucet to the keg coupler increases. Unfortunately, conditions can quickly arise in which the native state of carbonation in the keg is exceeded. In other words, more CO_2 pressure can be applied on the cold keg than is in the beer as the brewer packaged the keg, and this difference causes the carbonation in the keg to increase.

39. How much CO_2 is in a gas cylinder, and why is this independent of the applied pressure required for dispense?

CO_2 is measured in pounds loaded into cylinders, and cylinders come in several sizes. For low-pressure dispense, approximately 5/8 lb of CO_2 is required in a leak-free system. A 20-lb cylinder should dispense approximately 32 kegs.

A 20-lb gas cylinder, when filled, contains a liquid "heel" as well as a gas phase, and the internal pressure is over 800 psig (depending on the amount filled and the ambient temperature). Professionals never overfill gas cylinders, because the pressure can easily exceed the safety pressure relief threshold. During dispense, the gas is removed, and some of the liquid phase is converted to the gaseous form. Even when the entire heel is depleted, the cylinder maintains 800 psig, and the cylinder pressure begins to drop only when most of the gas is depleted. A regulator can work efficiently and accurately with a minimum feed pressure, typically 100 psig. Most of the gas is consumed by the time the cylinder pressure drops that low.

40. How many kegs can be dispensed per cylinder of mixed gas and per cylinder of CO_2?

A 20-lb aluminum cylinder of 60:40 mixed gas at 1,800 psig can dispense 25 to 30 half-barrel kegs. A 20-lb CO_2 cylinder pressurized to 875 psig (normal) can move 32 half-barrel kegs of beer through a short draw box at low pressure (e.g., 13 psig). The difference results from the fact that the 60:40 mix is not able to include a liquid heel; the cylinder contains compressed gas phase mixture only.

41. When is bulk CO_2 an alternative to cylinders?

A bulk tank is a stainless steel tank (typically approximately 3 ft in diameter and 4 ft high) holding 300 lb of CO_2. It is filled from the street as needed or as scheduled. The tank and hookup can be either leased or purchased.

If an account is using eight to ten 20-lb cylinders of CO_2 a month, then it is considerably cheaper to purchase bulk delivery CO_2 and load it into a leased stainless steel bulk tank. Bulk tanks vent 4% a day, so there is a minimum use requirement and the system cannot be prevented from venting. This is not a concern with gas cylinders.

42. How do secondary regulators help fine-tune the balancing on individual beer dispense lines?

CO_2 pressure can be throttled by regulators. This is important because many installations have several bars, and one bar closer to the walk-in cooler probably will require dispense at a lower pressure than a bar farther away. Also, different carbonation levels in beer require that different internal keg pressures be maintained, so it is possible for a product with low carbonation to be maintained with lower internal pressure when a secondary regulator is installed for that keg. *Figure 3.7* illustrates a simple means by which a secondary regulator allows a second keg to be dispensed with a different dispense pressure.

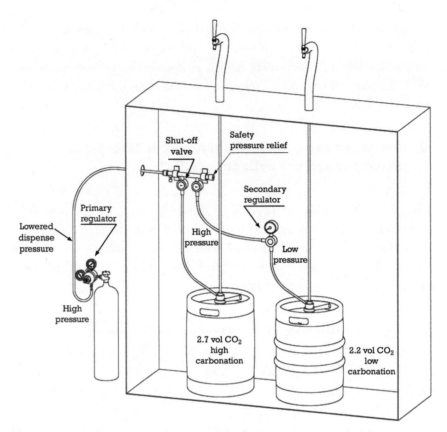

Figure 3.7. A well-placed secondary regulator allows a keg of lower target carbonation to be dispensed alongside one of higher carbonation.

43. Why do gas regulators whine sometimes?

Noise from a gas regulator may be caused by a torn diaphragm, which needs replacement. A regulator under a heavy load may freeze up and whine, and in this situation a high-volume regulator should be used.

A whine can also be caused by a sticky check valve or by internal valve noise as CO_2 passes through the regulator. To stop the whining, the valve on the CO_2 cylinder should be closed, disconnecting the regulator from the kegs. The pressure is set to 60 psig, and separate discharges of CO_2 are released. Then the adjustment is backed out, the CO_2 tank is reopened, and the adjustment screw is turned in and out to release the gas at lower pressure of few times. The system is then reset at normal dispense pressure.

44. What safety points are important for gases used in draft dispense?

At installation and annually, careful checking for leaks is required in any gas installation. The Compressed Gas Association warns that CO_2 concentrations of 15% cause unconsciousness in less than 1 minute. Nitrogen is also heavier than air, so in closed environs, the use of a gas monitor is absolutely required; this is needed for typical basement installations.

It is appropriate to install an "at-use" filter in a CO_2 line, as a last chance to ensure the purity of the gas before it reaches the keg. A CO_2 cylinder could have a rusty interior, and rust flakes must be kept from beer.

Additionally, food-grade CO_2 sometimes carries trace impurities, such as alcohol vapor, which may not affect the flavor of the beer, or hydrogen sulfide and acetaldehyde traces, which may. Simple cartridge filters can be installed to guarantee gas integrity and quality.

For systems in which nitrogen produced in-house is used, it is wise to install a quality filter that removes water and oil from the compressed air feed, followed by a sterile air filter. No filtration is recommended on the nitrogen gas outlet.

45. Why should I consider using mixed gas?

In some installations, particularly longer ones, the pressure required to yield a satisfactory dispense is higher than the internal keg pressure (equilibrium pressure of beer at a given temperature). If pure CO_2 is used, the beer in the keg may be exposed to higher CO_2 pressure—and the keg will carbonate above and beyond its brewery specification. Adding a low-solubility neutral gas allows the partial pressure from the CO_2 to be decreased.

46. What steps are used to determine the gas blend needed for an installation?

Using *Table 3.5* or specific brewery-supplied information on carbonation of a beer, we can ascertain the internal pressure of the keg in question at the temperature at which it will be held. In some installations, the necessary pressure required for dispense is not more than 3 or 4 psig above internal pressure. In some longer installations, a greater applied pressure is required and the use of a specific gas blend allows carbonation to be maintained, while also providing the motive force to properly dispense the beer from the faucet.

Table 3.5. Desired keg pressure at various volumes of CO_2 and beer temperatures

Temperature (°F)	Specialty and craft-brewed ales					Most beers						High-carbonation beers			
	1.8	2.0	2.1	2.2	2.3	2.4	2.5	2.6	2.7	2.8	2.9	3.0	3.1	3.2	3.3
32	1.6	3.5	4.4	5.4	6.3	7.3	8.2	9.2	10.1	11.0	12.0	12.9	13.9	14.8	15.7
33	1.9	3.9	4.9	5.8	6.8	7.8	8.7	9.7	10.6	11.6	12.6	13.5	14.5	15.4	16.4
34	2.3	4.3	5.3	6.3	7.3	8.2	9.2	10.2	11.2	12.1	13.1	14.1	15.1	16.0	17.0
35	2.7	4.7	5.7	6.7	7.7	8.7	9.7	10.7	11.7	12.7	13.7	14.7	15.7	16.7	17.7
36	3.1	5.1	6.2	7.2	8.2	9.2	10.2	11.2	12.3	13.3	14.3	15.3	16.3	17.3	18.3
37	3.5	5.6	6.6	7.6	8.7	9.7	10.7	11.8	12.8	13.8	14.9	15.9	16.9	17.9	18.9
38	3.9	6.0	7.0	8.1	9.1	10.2	11.2	12.3	13.3	14.4	15.4	16.5	17.5	18.6	19.6
39	4.3	6.4	7.5	8.6	9.6	10.7	11.8	12.8	13.9	15.0	16.0	17.1	18.1	19.2	20.2
40	4.7	6.8	7.9	9.0	10.1	11.2	12.3	13.4	14.4	15.5	16.6	17.7	18.8	19.8	20.9
41	5.1	7.3	8.4	9.5	10.6	11.7	12.8	13.9	15.0	16.1	17.2	18.3	19.4	20.5	21.6
42	5.5	7.7	8.8	10.0	11.1	12.2	13.3	14.4	15.5	16.7	17.8	18.9	20.0	21.1	22.2
43	5.9	8.1	9.3	10.4	11.6	12.7	13.8	15.0	16.1	17.2	18.4	19.5	20.6	21.7	22.9
44	6.3	8.6	9.7	10.9	12.1	13.2	14.4	15.5	16.7	17.8	19.0	20.1	21.3	22.4	23.5
45	6.7	9.0	10.2	11.4	12.5	13.7	14.9	16.1	17.2	18.4	19.6	20.7	21.9	23.0	24.2
46	7.1	9.5	10.7	11.8	13.0	14.2	15.4	16.6	17.8	19.0	20.2	21.3	22.5	23.7	24.9
47	7.5	9.9	11.1	12.3	13.5	14.7	15.9	17.2	18.4	19.6	20.8	22.0	23.2	24.3	25.5
48	7.9	10.4	11.6	12.8	14.0	15.3	16.5	17.7	18.9	20.1	21.4	22.6	23.8	25.0	26.2
49	8.3	10.8	12.0	13.3	14.5	15.8	17.0	18.3	19.5	20.7	22.0	23.2	24.4	25.7	26.9
50	8.7	11.3	12.5	13.8	15.0	16.3	17.6	18.8	20.1	21.3	22.6	23.8	25.1	26.3	27.6
51	9.1	11.7	13.0	14.3	15.5	16.8	18.1	19.4	20.6	21.9	23.2	24.5	25.7	27.0	28.2
52	9.6	12.2	13.5	14.8	16.1	17.3	18.6	19.9	21.2	22.5	23.8	25.1	26.4	27.6	28.9
53	10.0	12.6	13.9	15.3	16.6	17.9	19.2	20.5	21.8	23.1	24.4	25.7	27.0	28.3	29.6
54	10.4	13.1	14.4	15.7	17.1	18.4	19.7	21.1	22.4	23.7	25.0	26.3	27.7	29.0	30.3
55	10.8	13.5	14.9	16.2	17.6	18.9	20.3	21.6	23.0	24.3	25.6	27.0	28.3	29.7	31.0

Desired keg pressure (psig) at volumes of CO_2 in:

Table 3.5 also presents data on the pressure that must be maintained on beer in order to maintain specific carbonation and from which intermediate points can be interpolated. The carbonation level, in volumes of CO_2 (reading across the table), is matched with the beer temperature (reading down the first column), and the matching point in the table provides the gauge pressure that must be applied to maintain carbonation. For example, beer containing 2.65 volumes of CO_2 has an internal pressure of 11 psig at 35°F, 12.7 psig at 38.5°F, and 13.9 psig at 40°F.

The graphical tool shown in *Figure 3.8* can be used to determine the blend for a 38°F beer at various dispense pressures. The horizontal axis represents the applied keg pressure. Quantification of this requirement for application in the field is discussed later.

47. Should I look at nitrogen generators or nitrogen bulk systems?

Good design of a dispense system generally includes a review of the gas dispense options. Long-distance installations often benefit from mixed gas instead of pure CO_2 as the dispense medium. Many cities have vendors who sell premixed combinations of CO_2 and N_2 at a couple of different ratios. A nitrogen bulk tank or nitrogen generator can never be used on its own; a quality blender is needed to combine the nitrogen with CO_2 at the desired levels for the installation.

A rule of thumb is that if an account is going through more than eight kegs a week, it makes sense to look at the choices and costs. A bulk nitrogen tank, which is refilled on site, must vent regular amounts of nitrogen (3% a day). Not only is this a loss, but in a closed environment it introduces a health hazard. Liquid nitrogen is stored in insulated dewars to keep it liquid at modest pressures (200–300 psig).

When leasing or purchasing a nitrogen generator, one must remember that it requires a source of clean compressed air (often a dedicated compressor) and that there are noise and heat factors to consider. It is important to specify the maximum number of beers being drawn during peak hours to make sure the system is appropriately sized. A nitrogen generator uses either a membrane or pressure swing absorption to make a stream that is 99.7% nitrogen from air.

Although not typically part of a purchased or leased nitrogen generation system, it is highly recommended that two filters be inserted into the compressed-air feed line: one to remove tramp water or oil followed by a sterile air filter.

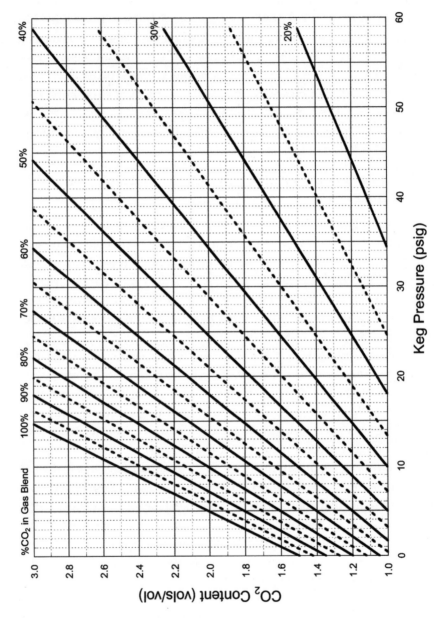

Figure 3.8. Gas-blend selection chart for beer stored at 38°F (3°C). (Courtesy of McDantim, Inc. Reprinted from Jurado, 2003b)

48. What are beer pumps, and when should they be used?

A beer pump is an option in dispense that often makes good sense as an alternative to mixed gases or nitrogen generators—a viable solution for long draw systems. A modest CO_2 pressure is applied on the kegs just to drive the beer to a pump located inside the cold box. The pump is fed by compressed air, CO_2, or a mixed-gas blend and pumps the beer through the beer line to the faucet. The compressed air or CO_2 driving gas is regulated, and increasing air pressure on the pump increases the beer flow rate through the line.

In terms of cost, a pneumatically driven beer pump is competitive with mixed-gas installations and is a cheaper option in terms of initial costs compared with a nitrogen-generation system and gas blender.

49. What is optimal for dispensing beer from serving tanks?

Beer pumps offer optimal dispense solutions for dispense from tanks larger than a keg for several reasons. Generally, it takes more time to deplete the beer from a serving tank than from a keg, so the beer in the tank must maintain its target carbonation level for a longer period.

Use of a pneumatic pump to deliver the beer allows the serving tank design to just maintain proper carbonation on the beer in the serving tank. A small excess pressure may be applied, which adds to the pressure head on the beer in the tank and which delivers beer smoothly to the beer pump. A beer pump is always on demand and activates the moment the faucet is opened.

50. What is series dispense, and how is the system cleaned?

At special events and in busy establishments where access to the cold box is a problem, kegs can be arranged in a series to extend the time between keg replacements. Essentially, beer from a keg that receives dispense gas is moved through another keg. Several kegs can be hooked in such an arrangement. The keg coupler must be adapted for such special duty, because beer moves into a keg via the gas inlet port. The Thompson check valve must be removed, and a 3/8-in. jumper hose must feed into it beer from the keg closer to the gas feed for the system.

Cleaning is more challenging than in single-keg systems. Intermediate taps and jumpers must be carefully and regularly cleaned, using special hardware fittings such as cleaning cups. Furthermore, the kegs in the series must be monitored and pulled out and replenished. The kegs must be rotated regularly, so that those last in line from the gas inlet are moved to the front of the line.

51. What flow rate should be targeted in pouring beer from a faucet?

The target flow rate is 2 oz per second (1 U.S. gallon per minute) in a quiescent pour. The rate can be increased for high-volume accounts and reduced for complex beers, but the typical faucet in North America has a fairly tight operating band allowing approximately 1 gallon per minute. Faucets with a smaller bore can be purchased from European vendors to additionally reduce the flow rate for "presentation" dispense, for example, into specialty glassware.

52. What is the simplest draft installation?

The simplest installation is the direct draw box, a refrigerated box, often set at 38°F (3°C), with a very short line between the keg coupler and the faucet. At 38°F, the internal pressure in the keg is 12 psig, and a working dispense pressure of 14–15 psig generally works very well to gently transport the beer.

53. Line resistance/restriction: Rules of thumb?

Restriction is another word for friction. Friction is a consequence of wall shear that occurs naturally when fluid is transported through a pipe or tube. The smaller the inner diameter (ID), the greater the wall shear and the greater the restriction.

Restriction is a tool for the draft dispense system designer and installer. By adding small-bore tubing to a line, one can add restriction, and by removing existing small-bore line, one can decrease restriction. Small-bore line, or choker line, is normally 3/16-in. ID, but good success has been achieved with 1/6-in.-ID line, which offers greater restriction.

Restriction can be added in various situations, for example, to decrease flow through a faucet. *Table 3.6* is a useful guideline. To slow flow from 115 to 100 oz/min, 4 psig of restriction is added, and approximately 2 ft of choker line is required to increase restriction by 4 psig.

Restriction from added choker is only one parameter of a draft installation. (See following examples on balancing lines.)

54. What is the resistance caused by the beer dispense line, and is this the only restriction we must overcome in dispensing beer?

Restriction of beer dispense line is dependent on its inside diameter. There is also restriction from the keg coupler, from the faucet, from bends in the line, and often from other components in the dispense line. Beer line offers the most resistance. Average values are provided in *Table 3.7,* but manufacturers can provide accurate restriction data for their specific lines.

55. How do I balance a draft system?

There are various rigorous approaches to balancing and designing a draft dispense system. Calculation methodologies include factors accounting for altitude, desired rate of pour, temperature differentials, and specific hardware-component restriction data. A robust starting-point approach is illustrated here. There are good workbook tools to address specific parts of this issue, such as how to calculate restriction needed to adjust dispense flow rates.

The pressure on the beer regulator gauge must be set to equal the pounds of resistance calculated in the formula below. *Table 3.5* lists desired keg pressures for different CO_2 volumes at different temperatures. The brewery representative can provide the true carbonation level. For

Table 3.6. Line restrictions and faucet flow rates

	Flow rate (oz/min)	Restriction to be added (psig)
High	128	0
Normal	115	3
Low	100	7

Table 3.7. Restriction in beer lines made of different materials

Inside diameter (in.)	Line restriction (psi per foot) in beer lines made of:			
	Vinyl	Polyethylene	Barrier-lined tube	Stainless steel
3/16	2.2–3.0	2.2	. . .	. . .
1/4	0.6–0.85	0.40–0.50	0.30	0.66
5/16	0.2–0.3	0.10–0.15	. . .	. . .
3/8	0.10–0.15	0.06–0.07	0.06	0.084
1/2	0.025	. . .	. . .	. . .

example, if the carbonation level is 2.6 vol at 38°F, the required keg pressure (from the chart) is 12.3 psig.

The regulator setting (gauge) pressure is calculated as follows:

$$\text{Regulator pressure} = (\text{Length of beer line} \times \text{Line resistance}) + (\text{Lift} \times 0.5)$$

where

> the length of the beer line is measured in feet
> line resistance is the total resistance (using specific resistance of each part of the beer line run from *Table 3.7*)
> lift is the height in feet of the faucet above the keg connector or serving tank
> regulator pressure is applied pressure from the CO_2 cylinder

Example 1 (*Figure 3.9*). The faucet is 5 ft above the keg, and the beer line is 3 ft of 1/4-in. polyvinyl jumper line followed by 10 ft of 1/4-in. barrier tube, followed by 3 ft of 3/16-in. polyethylene choker tubing. The total resistance is

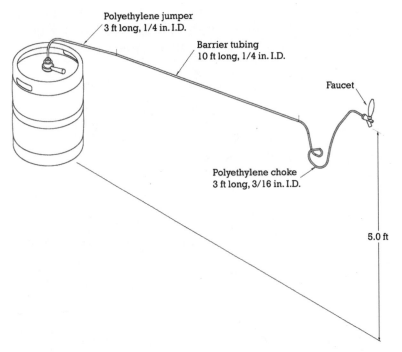

Figure 3.9. Example 1.

$$(3 \text{ ft} \times 0.85 \text{ lb/ft}) + (10 \text{ ft} \times 0.30 \text{ lb/ft})$$

$$+ (3 \text{ ft} \times 2.2 \text{ lb/ft}) + (5 \text{ ft} \times 0.5 \text{ lb/ft})$$

$$= (2.55 \text{ lb}) + (3 \text{ lb}) + (6.6 \text{ lb}) + (2.5 \text{ lb})$$

$$= 14.65 \text{ lb}$$

Conclusion: Set the regulator at 15 lb.

Example 2 (*Figure 3.10*).   The faucet is 4 ft above the keg base, and the beer line is 7 ft of 3/16-in. polyvinyl line. The total resistance is

$$(7 \text{ ft} \times 2.7 \text{ lb/ft}) + (4 \text{ ft} \times 0.5 \text{ lb/ft})$$

$$= (18.9 \text{ lb}) + (2.0 \text{ lb})$$

$$= 20.9 \text{ lb}$$

Conclusion: Set the regulator at 21 lb. Note that this pressure is considerably higher than 12.3 psig, which is the pressure required to maintain carbonation! A larger-bore trunk line will reduce the restriction and therefore reduce the delivery pressure required. (Also see questions that discuss pneumatic pumps and mixed gas to review how these options make

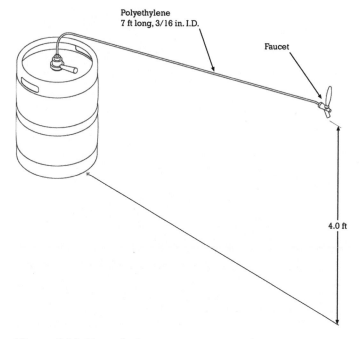

Figure 3.10. Example 2.

preservation of specified carbonation in the beer being dispensed in this line practical.)

56. How is the length of the beer line used to adjust restriction?

An easy rule to determine the ideal length of a beer line is to start with the ideal pressure (internal pressure needed to meet the CO_2 target at the dispense temperature), add 5 psig, and then divide by the restriction of the line per linear foot. If the beer pours too slowly, shorten the line as needed.

57. How is restriction adjusted with chokers?

Adding a choker slows beer pouring speed and helps inhibit foaming. For a highly carbonated cloudy Belgian wheat beer, it is not uncommon to find that 25 ft or more of choker is required to settle the pour in a system of low resistance. Typically, choker is applied as close to the faucet as possible, and keeping the loop as cold as possible is mandated.

58. How is the required gas blend determined? What is the mixed-gas calculation?

Using *Table 3.5* or specific brewery-supplied information on carbonation of a beer, we ascertain the internal pressure of the keg in question at the keg beer temperature.

In example 2 above, 21 psig is needed to overcome resistance, but 12.3 psig is the internal pressure; 12.3 psig of the applied pressure should come from CO_2, and the balance should come from N_2.

In calculating the required blend, the absolute pressure must be used. It is calculated as follows for sea level installations:

$$\text{Absolute pressure} = \text{Gauge pressure} + 14.7$$

Therefore, the blend required is

$$\% \ CO_2 = [(12.3 + 14.7)/(21 + 14.7)] \times 100 = 76\%$$

$$\% \ N_2 = 100\% - 76\% = 24\%$$

59. How should the glass be handled during the pour?

The head on a beer, its foam, is controlled by the angle of the beer as it enters the glass. To increase the foaminess of a pour, the glass is held more upright. To keep foam to a controlled minimum, the pour is started with the glass held at an angle toward the faucet.

60. What is a good technique for pouring beer?

The tap handle is grasped at its base, and the faucet is opened all the way with a quick, smooth motion. Pulling the tap handle at the top opens the faucet more slowly, and the beer might draw foamy. When a standard North American faucet is used, the glass should not be allowed to touch the faucet. The glass is tilted slightly (not more than 45 degrees) at the beginning of the pour and straightened as the pour continues. The glass should be topped with a collar of 1/2 to 1 in. of foam.

61. What is the objective of cleaning glassware?

Glassware is cleaned not only to sanitize it but also to keep it visually bright, free of nonrinsing deposits, blemishes, and film. Water spotting, streaking, lipstick residues, and even fingerprints can be readily seen if glassware is held against bright light and are some of the telltale signs of incorrect washing.

62. How should glassware be cleaned?

Cleaning glasses in warm water with beer-clean (brewery-approved) detergent followed by a clean, cold water rinse is common for manual cleaning as well as machine cleaning in specialized cabinet glass-washers. In the United States, a final sanitation step is also required because glasses are contacted by both hands and mouths. Chemical sterilants must be free-rinsing and must not leave odors when the surfaces dry. Glass-washers use hot water possibly followed by air blowing for rapid drying. The final step in preparing glasses is air drying on clean, raised drying surfaces that promote airflow inside the glasses.

63. What tests can be used to determine whether glassware is "beer clean"?

If beer is poured into a glass and the foam rapidly collapses or if small bubbles are readily seen distributed over its inner surface, the glass is not "beer clean."

The water-break test is one method for determining whether glassware is sufficiently clean. A cleaned glass is fully immersed in clean water and then removed, allowing all the water to run out. If the water sheets off and does not leave drops on the surface, then the glass is probably beer clean.

Another method is the salt test, in which granulated salt is evenly shaken across the entire internal (wetted) surface. Salt adheres to a glass surface that is pristine.

Table 3.8. Water hardness (grains per gallon)

Soft water	<1
Slightly hard water	1–3.5
Moderately hard water	3.5–7
Hard water	7–10.5
Very hard water	10.5+

64. Is there a simple water hardness test for use in taverns and other licensed accounts?

The simplest test to determine water hardness is to add drops of liquid soap to 28 ml (1 oz) of water. The number of drops required to produce a scum of soap equals the grains per gallon. A simple hardness scale is given by *Table 3.8.* Hard water requires softening.

65. How should a manual glass-washing station be managed?

To make sure glasses are beer clean, a three-sink cleaning system is ideal. The first sink is for washing the glasses, the second for rinsing, and the third for sanitizing (sanitizing is required in the United States). If only a two-sink system is available, the first is used for cleaning the glasses and the second for sanitizing.

Staff should always use cleaners and sanitizers specifically designed for cleaning beer glasses, and air should be allowed inside the glasses during drying. It is usually best to use a drying rack. Before beer is poured into a glass, it should be rinsed with cold water whenever possible.

The glass-washing brushes should be cleaned regularly. A simple protocol is to boil the brushes in clean water containing 4 tablespoons of table salt per gallon. Special detergents for cleaning and soaking the brushes can also be purchased.

66. Any comments on frosted glasses?

The use of glass-cooling equipment can allow draft beer to be poured and delivered in top form, but freezing glassware creates obvious problems: frosting and ice formation. Both negatively affect foam. One also encounters "shocked" beer, where clear-poured beer from the faucet becomes foamy because of the temperature difference between the beer and the ice in the glass. Keeping glasses at 36°F (2°C) in a chill cabinet or using an attemperated water spray just before filling are ideal ways to prepare the glass. Rinsing an iced glass in water before filling also works well.

Figure 3.11. Oily water in a dispense gas line.

67. What are the parameters of the cabinet- or well-style glass chiller?

A regular glass cooler chills the environment to approximately 15°F (–9°C) by using a closed refrigerant such as 405 in a 1/3-HP compressor loop typically operating at a suction of 15 psig. Glasses are loaded at room temperature (or warmer), and the dew point of air is reached (and then surpassed as the temperature continues to drop) so that an even condensation of vapor creates frosting across all glass surfaces.

Good presentations of draft in iced glasses are possible if care is taken during pour to achieve adequate foaming.

68. What causes flat beer in a draft dispense application?

Over time, if the gas applied to the keg is insufficiently balanced (as might happen if a blend of 25% CO_2 + 75% N_2 is applied to a "regular" lager), the keg can decarbonate. Flat pours can also occur when the beer is too cold or flows too slowly into the glass at the faucet or when it is dispensed into glassware that is not beer clean.

Oil leakage and contamination in gas lines used in draft dispense can also affect carbonation (*Figure 3.11*).

Figure 3.12. Secondary regulator check hardware.

69. What causes cloudy beer in a draft dispense application?

Cloudy pours can occur when the dispense hardware has not been properly cleaned, when the glassware has been poorly cleaned, or when the beer has previously frozen and precipitated a proteinaceous chill haze.

70. What causes foamy beer in a draft dispense application?

Foaming commonly occurs when the beer is warm, either because of a problem in the cold box or through heat pickup in the dispense line, or because it is poured into a warm glass. Other causes include the following:

a. **Carbonation** in the keg has increased over time because the equilibrium pressure of CO_2 was exceeded by the gas pressure on the keg or the applied pressure is too low to properly overcome the resistance in the dispense line.

b. **Kinked beer line** can cause venturi-related flashing.

c. **Beer stone deposits** in the line can create rough surfaces that cause foam to break out.

d. **Worn couplers** that are loose and do not completely seal and chopped or torn keg valve gaskets also cause foamy pours.

e. **A freshly delivered keg** is much livelier than a keg that has not been shaken for some period.

f. **Faulty secondary regulator,** which can be checked with a pressure tester (*Figure 3.12*).

A high dispense temperature, a just-emptied keg, poor technique in pouring the beer, excessive dispense pressure, a kinked line, and a hot spot in the line are all common reasons for foamy pours.

71. What causes flashing foam in beer?

More often than not, foam problems are caused by warm beer. If the temperature of the beer is not the source of the problem, then several alternative causes can be explored.

"Flashing foam" is intermittent inclusions of a foamy interface in beer poured from the faucet. The result is foamy beer in the glass with an excessively large foam collar on top. The first thing to check is that the keg coupler is appropriately engaged. The coupler should then be removed, inspected, rinsed, and reengaged. The keg valve it mates to should also be inspected and rinsed. Before the coupler is reconnected, the beer faucet should be removed, disassembled, and cleaned, and the vent holes and all surfaces in contact with beer should be cleaned. The faucet is then rebuilt and reattached, and the keg is reconnected. Applied pressure is then checked. If the pressure has dropped, foam breakout might be occurring in the dispense line. If no apparent agitation has occurred in the keg that might offer a second concern (the first being that the keg was recently delivered and not yet sufficiently cooled), then one needs to look for another cause, such as restriction in the dispense system. Finally, the problem may be a keg with a faulty seal, so a different keg should be attached. If the new keg pours well, then isolate the problem keg and call the appropriate salesperson.

72. In dispense from a Hoff-Stevens keg, what causes foamy beer if the dispense temperature and pressure are correct?

A worn beer coupler may have internal washers that have expanded to create a partial blockage. The figure-eight washer on the probe should be checked to see whether it has split, causing dispense gas to mix with beer and create foamy beer at the admixture point. The lock threads and probes should also be inspected. If the probes are worn and not full length, they will constrict the keg opening. If the threads are worn or corroded, the keg may not be pierced completely by the probes, again creating a restriction inside the keg.

Cracking of the nylon down tube in a Hoff-Stevens keg can cause problems. Beer in the keg above the crack will pour normally, but when

Figure 3.13. Flow-of-beer (FOB) stop detector prevents accidental emptying of the beer line.

the surface level of the beer is below the crack, the gas in the keg enters the crack and mixes with beer in the tube, creating a wild, foamy dispense.

Finally, the temperature of the beer in the keg and exiting the faucet should be rechecked.

73. What effect does a bad Thomas valve have on a Hoff-Stevens keg?

Despite the oft-heard assertion that a bad check valve (Thomas valve) in a Hoff-Stevens keg coupler causes wild beer, this is not the case. The check valve prevents beer from a Hoff-Stevens keg from backing up into the gas pressure line—it protects the regulator. Even without a Thomas valve, the beer will draw perfectly.

74. What can be done to prevent flooding a beer dispense line with foam when a keg is emptied?

The flow-of-beer (FOB) stop detector is a proven piece of hardware that incorporates a simple float (*Figure 3.13*). When a keg is empty, the

Figure 3.14. Flow-of-beer (FOB) stop detectors in a high-volume, multiple-tap venue. (Courtesy of The Porterhouse, London)

chamber empties, the beer in the FOB empties, and the float drops and seals all beer in the dispense line. This allows a simple keg changeover, easy bleeding, and reestablishment of flow without filling the beer dispense line with foam.

75. Should every installation have a FOB?

FOBs introduce a new complexity to an installation, present new maintenance challenges, and also require due attention during line cleaning. Therefore, short-draw systems (less than 15 ft) are not candidates for FOB installation. In high-volume accounts, such as the one shown in *Figure 3.14,* with many long lines and high keg volume, FOBs make good sense.

76. What can be done when installing a FOB to alleviate concerns about cleanliness?

Use of hygienic connections and a plumbed drain line for bleeding makes FOB installation simple. Quick-release couplings allow periodic removal for manual internal cleaning.

77. Why is the traditional dispense of British-style ales different from that of normal kegs?

The heritage and traditions of cask-conditioned ale influence its dispense. The important process occurring in the cask is natural carbonation by secondary fermentation, and often the brewer adds finings and priming sugar to the cask. Production protocols of special ales that undergo secondary fermentation in the cask are discussed in Volume 2, Chapter 3.

Cask dispense has an approach different from that of modern draft dispense and its own unique hardware. There are two methods of gas displacement of cask beer, traditional dispense and the use of a cask breather, but each is designed to preserve the natural carbonation in the ale inside the cask at the level achieved by secondary fermentation. Mechanical carbonation is to be avoided.

The most common cask size is the 9-gallon (U.K.) firkin (10.8 U.S. gallons) Traditional cask-conditioned ale dispense removes ale from the cask and allows air to enter as ale is removed. This, of course, allows oxidation and very slow decarbonation to commence. Once ale withdrawal begins, traditional dispense allows consumption of a cask in less than 3 days before noticeable differences in flavor result. Following recommendations of specific breweries, the cask is normally vented (in some cases, at least 24 hours prior to tapping) to allow for the subtle oxidation that brings in additional, subtle flavor notes and quiets the beer.

The use of a cask breather, a system that permits low-pressure CO_2 to enter the cask as ale is withdrawn, allows many more venues to serve cask-conditioned ale. The CO_2 is admitted at a pressure very slightly above normal ambient pressure to minimize any undesirable infusion of CO_2 into the ale. Such dispense can double the life of a cask, making what otherwise might be a marginal or risky offering for a particular retailer a viable sales option.

In most situations, the carbonation level of cask-conditioned ales is lower than that of their kegged, bottled, and canned brethren. Once in the cellar, cask-conditioned ales benefit from a period of storage (stillaging) before being served.

78. What modes of dispense are appropriate for cask-conditioned ales?

The oldest option is simply gravity dispense; that is, the cask is emptied by drawing the ale through a faucet and the static pressure of ale in the cask gently forces the ale out. Ambient air displaces the withdrawn ale. Gravity dispense offers the gentlest pour possible. The beer engine (hand pump) is the most common dispense, but the pneumatic driven (isolated) pump and electric pump represent acceptable options. CO_2 or mixed gas to drive ale from cask to glass is not used—top pressure must be avoided in dispense. Some controversy exists in the United Kingdom about the appropriateness of the cask-breather (mistakenly called an aspirator in some places). The traditional cask-conditioned ale aficionado more often than not rejects that hardware component. In North America, there is no similar consumer resistance.

79. What is the purpose of fining, and how is it used?

For secondary fermentation to occur in the cask, the brewer allows yeast to be carried through with the ale. The yeast converts fermentable sugar to CO_2, but it also causes cloudiness. If the brewery wants its cask-conditioned ales to appear as bright and brilliant as possible, the brewer adds finings to each cask. Finings attract yeast and agglomerate into flocs, which settle to the bottom of the cask, leaving bright and uncloudy ale above. Cloudy or turbid beers are not tolerated by pub customers in the United Kingdom, and brilliant clarity is as much a concern to the cask ale brewer as the flavor of the beer. See Chapter 1, Volume 2, for further discussion.

80. What is priming sugar?

Priming sugar is fermentable sugar added to a cask, which is then tightly sealed, to provide the nutrition required by the yeast present in solution to ferment and carbonate the ale. Traditionalists argue that carbonation of the ale in cask allows for the most delicate flavors to result.

81. What hardware is commonly found in casks used for cask-conditioned ale?

Simple cask hardware is shown in *Figure 3.15*. Terminology varies, depending on location: *spile* and *spike* are interchangeable with *peg*, for example. The cask itself looks different from a keg. By design, the cask is rested on its side in horizontal orientation, to promote the settlement of sediment in its belly.

82. What does cask breather hardware look like, and how is it installed?

A cask breather set consists of the breather spile (plastic construction); a nonreturn valve, which prevents beer or foam from flowing backward through the set; and a regulated gas cylinder. *Figure 3.16* shows one type of cask breather, which admits low-pressure CO_2 into a cask as ale is displaced. Gas enters at 3 psig or lower.

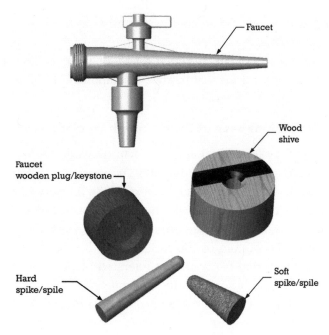

Figure 3.15. Hardware used for tapping and serving cask ale. The faucet is pounded through the faucet wooden plug (or keystone) to tap the cask. The shive (or bung) contains a drilled hole to allow a soft spike or hard spike to be seated and regulate gas release from the beer.

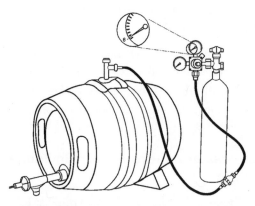

Figure 3.16. Cask breather system attached to the wood shive in place of a soft or hard spike. The cask breather is set at a very low counter pressure. Note the in-line filter on the gas line. (Reprinted, by permission, from Jurado 2003c)

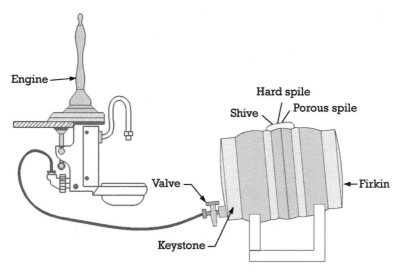

Figure 3.17. Traditional cask installation with the stillaged cask tipped slightly forward. The faucet is tapped through the keystone and connected to the beer engine by a length of tubing. (Reprinted, by permission, from Jurado 2003c)

83. What does a traditional cask-conditioned ale dispense installation look like?

Figure 3.17 illustrates the traditional setup. The cask has either a soft spile or hard spile in place, an outlet valve, and a line running to a beer engine, or hand pump. Unique features include a means to tilt the cask to fully drain it without disturbing the layer of fine sediment deposited on the bottom.

A hard wood spile seals the cask, and a soft wood peg allows CO_2 to escape. By alternating spiles, a professional server ("cellarman" is the traditional title) can control the natural carbonation of the beer.

84. What are the components of a hand pump, and what do they do?

The traditional hand pump (or beer engine) is affixed to a suction pump. When the handle is pulled, a half-pint is drawn into the glass. The workings of a typical hand pump are shown in *Figure 3.18.* In lieu of a faucet, the outlet is a small-diameter, swan-necked spout in the shape of a hairpin. It serves to shoot ale into the glass, mix the contents, and create foam in the ale. A swan neck might also have a sparkler at its outlet, which squirts the ale through a nozzle containing small holes to increase foaming.

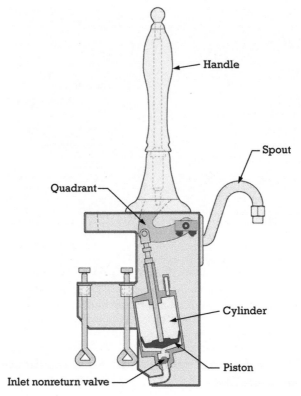

Figure 3.18. A typical beer engine. The pump cylinder and lever arm handle deliver one half-pint per pull through the swan-necked spout. The inlet nonreturn valve prevents beer from back-siphoning to the cask.

85. What is the purpose of the beer engine?

The beer engine provides the motive force to draw ale (a draught) from cask to glass. It is a simple manual pump that creates a slight vacuum in a cylinder, enough to pull ale up from the cask below. Traditional beer engines have large-bore tubing, to reduce friction (resistance) of the ale. The distance between the cask and the beer engine is limited.

86. How can cask-conditioned ale be served where there is long distance between the cask and the spout?

A cylinderless beer engine, which often features a demand valve at the base, can be used. When the handle is pulled, the valve opens and a pneumatic pump in the cellar propels the beer along the lines to the glass. Pneumatic beer pumps work instantly upon pressure drop at the pump outlet. Pulling the handle opens the line and drops the pressure, and the pump engages.

There are advantages to the cylinderless beer engine. There are few moving or mechanical parts. Small-bore lines mean less beer volume in transit between the cask and the outlet, making the product easy to cool and keep cool, because a small volume per linear foot is easier to keep cold.

87. What is the preferred serving temperature of cask-conditioned ale?

If real ale is too warm, it is not appealing, because it loses its "natural conditioning" (dissolved CO_2). On the other hand, if it is too cold, it does not express its subtle flavor. Generally, cask-conditioned ales should be served cool, at a temperature somewhat below ambient temperature, but generally warmer than kegged beer. The typical U.K. cellar temperature is 51–57°F (11–14°C).

88. How are beer engines cleaned?

Beer engines should be cleaned weekly to avoid buildups of yeast in the lines and pump cylinder. A typical cleaning regime might include the following:

a. A warm 1–2% solution of alkaline detergent is pulled through the lines and pump.
b. The solution is allowed to stand for 10–20 minutes or as directed by the detergent manufacturer.
c. The solution is recirculated for another 5 minutes.
d. The internal surface of the swan neck is cleaned with a flexible brush.
e. Rinse water at ambient temperature is pulled through the installation to flush out the lines and pump until litmus paper indicates neutral pH.
f. Exposed brass surfaces are polished with an approved brass cleaner.
g. The system is cleared of rinse water by pulling beer through the lines.

ACKNOWLEDGMENTS

C. Alvarez, president of The Gambrinus Company, is acknowledged for permission to publish this chapter. Patrick Magallanes, The Gambrinus Company, is thanked for providing photos, and Sohail Anwar is thanked for his assistance with graphics.

REFERENCES

Jurado, J. 2003a. Spick and span. *Brewers' Guardian* 132(5):16–20.

Jurado, J. 2003b. Hygienic design, installation, and maintenance standards for draft beer dispense: German progress and North America's challenge. *Technical Quarterly of the Master Brewers Association of the Americas* 40:271–279.

Jurado, J. 2003c. Ensuring quality draught dispense. *Brewers' Guardian* 132(12):20–23.

CHAPTER 4

Environmental Engineering

Fred Porter
New Belgium Brewing Company

Karl Ockert
BridgePort Brewing Company

1. What is environmental engineering?

The Environmental Engineering Division of the American Society of Civil Engineers (ASCE) has issued the following statement of purpose (Davis and Cornwell, 1991):

> Environmental engineering is manifest by sound engineering thought and practice in the solution of problems of environmental sanitation, notably in the provision of safe, palpable, and ample public water supplies; the proper disposal of or recycle of wastewater and solid wastes; the adequate drainage of urban and rural areas for proper sanitation; and the control of water, soil, and atmospheric pollution, and the social and environmental impact of these solutions. Furthermore it is concerned with engineering problems in the field of public health, such as control of arthropod-borne diseases, the elimination of industrial health hazards, and the provision of adequate sanitation in urban, rural, and recreational areas, and the effect of technological advances on the environment.

2. How does environmental engineering apply to the brewing industry?

While environmental engineering for a brewery does not encompass as broad a spectrum as that described above, there are still many environmental issues to be considered. This chapter focuses primarily on ideas for reducing the use of raw materials and reducing or reusing by-products of the brewing process. However, there are also several environmental concerns inside the brewery such as noise; heating, ventilation, air conditioning, and air quality; lighting; and building materials that should also be considered but are not discussed in this chapter. All of these areas have implications for both the interior environment of the brewery and the exterior environment. This chapter focuses solely on the exterior engineering considerations; interior concerns are covered in Chapter 1, Volume 3.

3. What impact does a brewery have on the environment?

The environment encompasses three major areas: land, air, and water. Brewing has an impact on every area of our environment. Breweries create many different types of solid waste, from marketing swag to brewing by-products such as spent grain and *kieselguhr* (diatomaceous earth, or DE). Volatile organic carbons (VOC) from the kettle boil, carbon dioxide from fermentation and packaging, and combustion waste from steam boilers are all released into the air. Perhaps the largest environmental impact and most costly waste stream is brewery wastewater. Management of all of these waste streams falls within the ASCE definition of environmental engineering, and each has several costs associated with it. If systems are properly engineered from the start, both the economic and environmental costs can be minimized. It is even possible to recover costs from waste by-products. The extent to which environmental impacts are evaluated and addressed depends on local and national legislation and the environmental values of the brewery management, which may also affect investment decisions.

3. When a brewery is considering the purchase of equipment to reduce environmental impacts, what payback period is optimal?

This is somewhat of a philosophical question. Return-on-investment considerations vary from one business to the next, and there may be overriding regulatory requirements or even marketing considerations as well. A standard payback period is five years, although the life expectancy of the equipment must also be considered. More important than the payback period should be these philosophical questions: How much is the reduction in emissions worth? Will we consider a longer payback period given greater environmental benefits? While five years is reasonable, some breweries may be willing to consider a longer payback period for equipment that has added environmental benefits. Whatever the payback period, these are important questions and should be among the first considerations. Many states have tax incentives to help increase the return on investment, especially in regard to energy.

4. What is the best approach to creating an environmentally friendly brewery?

It is best to look at the whole system prior to construction. However, since this is not possible for an existing brewery, an environmental audit can be performed for a brewery that is already in operation. There are several approaches to an audit. In a simple approach, the brewery should be viewed as a system with raw material entering and product and waste streams exiting. The first task is to determine a simple material-and-energy balance of the whole process. All raw materials and energy entering the facility as well as all waste streams exiting the facility must be accounted for, with flow rates determined for each stream. Raw material and waste stream metrics should be equated to a ratio based on production, to make it easy to scale up or down according to the rate of production.

5. When should a material balance be performed?

The material balance should be considered during the design phase. It is much easier and more cost effective to save raw materials from the beginning than to retrofit processes to reclaim waste streams. Efficiencies are often overlooked to keep up-front capital costs as low as possible. Brewing systems should be reviewed for use of raw materials and energy efficiency. When purchase of new equipment is planned, one of the first considerations should be its performance efficiency. Vendors should be able to guarantee specific efficiencies for their equipment, and tests should be performed immediately after installation and start-up to ensure that the equipment operates as promised.

Finally, after all raw materials have been optimized, waste streams must be considered and plans should be made for reuse and recycling wherever possible.

6. What standard raw materials should be accounted for in a material balance?

A material balance should include the following materials but may include others specific to the brewery's process:

Water
Grain

Hops
Kieselguhr (DE)
Filter pads, bags, etc.
Electricity
Natural gas
Steam
CO_2
Glass
Stretch wrap
Cardboard
Kegs
Marketing swag (e.g., T-shirts, glasses, and coasters)

7. What are the standard wastes from a brewery?

The following are examples of wastes and coproducts generated by a typical brewery:

Wastewater
Spent grain
Trub
Kieselguhr (DE) slurry
Other filter media wastes
Combustion gases from steam and electrical generation
Waste heat
CO_2 from fermentations and processing
Glass
Cardboard
Beer spillage, ullage
Marketing swag (e.g., T-shirts, glasses, and coasters)
Yeast, tank bottoms
Noise
Plastics

8. Where should energy be focused to provide the greatest overall environmental benefit?

Assuming that the raw material usage has been optimized, the next step is to look at the waste streams. The goal is to find simple solutions that do not require large capital outlay and major process changes. For example, switching from coal-fired electricity to an alternative energy source, such as wind or possibly hydropower, can reduce overall CO_2 emissions by as much as 33%. Wind-based energy results in a slight increase in operating cost, but there are no engineering or capital costs since the change involves only signing a contract with the utility company. This is important for the small start-up brewery that desires to be environmentally friendly but does not have the engineering resources and capital available to make large investments.

Rule of thumb: Look for the biggest return with the lowest capital costs and fewest equipment modifications, and then work up from there. For example, one simple change could be to use biodiesel fuel rather than diesel fuel in delivery vehicles.

9. What are some other methods of saving energy?

Other methods of saving energy include

> Insulating piping for hot and cold water, beer, clean-in-place (CIP), and steam and condensate
> Phasing in energy-efficient pumps
> Switching to ammonia-based refrigeration
> Installing energy-efficient lights and using natural lighting where possible
> Vaporizing CO_2 by using waste heat saved from kettle vapor, wastewater streams, and hot water makeup

After the easy changes are made, the next areas to focus on are the major cost centers. For most breweries, these are water usage, wastewater treatment, and solid waste disposal.

10. What types of air pollution are created by brewing?

There are several sources of air pollution from breweries, including

> Combustion gases and CO_2 from delivery vehicles
> Combustion gases from electrical generation
> Combustion gases from steam generation
> VOC from the kettle boil
> CO_2 from fermentation and processing
> Odors from the brewing process and waste products (e.g., spent grain, DE, and yeast)

11. What can be done to mitigate air pollution?

a. Delivery vehicles. Alternative fuels can be used in delivery vehicles. Biodiesel fuel, created from waste vegetable-based oils and animal fats, is probably the most practical choice for reducing pollution from delivery vehicles at this time, because it burns cleaner than diesel fuel. According to a study by the U.S. Environmental Protection Agency (EPA), carbon monoxide is reduced by 48%, hydrocarbons by at least 60%, and particulate matter by 45% when 100% biodiesel fuels are used (Environmental Protection Agency, 2002). These results were obtained by burning 100% biodiesel fuel, which is not always possible. There is no need for any engine modification, but use of biodiesel fuel results in a slight reduction in power, and the fuel is temperature sensitive. Blends of biodiesel and regular diesel fuels that remain stable at temperatures below 20°F (–7°C) are available in cold climates.

Hybrid cars, although not practical as delivery vehicles, make sense for use by salespeople and as lightweight errand vehicles.

b. Electrical generation.   Many utility companies offer alternative energy programs. Generating electricity with coal creates huge amounts of CO_2 emissions. Approximately 2.27 lb of CO_2 is released into the atmosphere for every kilowatt of electricity generated. This statistic is from the Platte River Power Authority, which operates a highly efficient and well-maintained coal plant. The CO_2 generated by coal-fired electrical generation supplying a 200,000-barrel-per-year brewery is 22 lb/bbl of beer produced, while the CO_2 generated by fermentation is 9.4 lb/bbl. By simply changing electrical generation fuel sources, a brewery can significantly reduce its CO_2 emissions. High-efficiency electric motors should be selected whenever possible to reduce operating costs and decrease energy consumption. These kinds of calculations will become more relevant as emission of "greenhouse gases," such as CO_2, becomes more highly regulated.

c. Steam generation.   Many fuels are used for steam generation; of these, natural gas is the cleanest. Boilers must be maintained regularly to ensure that the combustion ratio is optimal. This reduces both fuel costs and air pollution. Steam generators that use low volumes of water may be more space- and energy-efficient for small breweries.

d. VOC emissions.   Vapors from the brew kettle are a source of high-VOC emissions. A simple solution is to install a vapor condenser on the kettle. This will not only reduce VOC emissions but will also recover huge amounts of energy. Approximately 4 kWh can be saved for every hectoliter of cast wort. This energy can be stored in the form of hot water, which can be used for preheating wash water, for CO_2 vaporization, and even for heating buildings.

e. Fermentation CO_2.   The CO_2 produced by fermentation is approximately 15 lb/bbl (12°P wort). The first attempts at CO_2 recovery were made using the Nathan process with closed vessels and conical outlets (Kunze, 1996, p. 347). Despite the fact that CO_2 emissions are not yet regulated in the United States, CO_2 is considered a greenhouse gas and may contribute to global climate change. CO_2 recovery is a viable option. Not only can fermentation CO_2 be recovered, but in theory CO_2 could also be recovered from waste combustion gases (which contain considerable amounts of it) and used for wastewater neutralization.

Several manufacturers produce skid-mounted CO_2 recovery systems, which are capable of operating at flows as low as 88 lb per hour. This translates to a production rate of approximately 85,000 bbl per year (Heyse et al., 1996). The payback on a system like this varies and is heavily dependent on the cost and availability of CO_2 locally. *Figure 4.1* is a schematic diagram of a small skid-mounted recovery system.

12. What is the process for CO_2 recovery?

The process for CO_2 recovery is as follows (Union Engineering website, 2005; Kunze, 1996, pp. 393–394):

a. Foam separation.   Gas is bubbled through water to remove foam.

b. Scrubbing.   A gas scrubber removes water-soluble impurities.

c. Compression.   The gas is compressed to raise its pressure to 250 to 300 psi.

d. Drying.   The gas is dried, usually with a desiccant dryer.

e. Carbon filtration.   The gas is filtered to remove odors from compounds such as acetates, aldehydes, and sulfur compounds (notably dimethyl sulfide), which create off flavors.

f. Refrigeration.   Clean, dry CO_2 is refrigerated and liquefied.

g. Storage.   Liquid CO_2 is stored in a well-insulated tank.

13. What CO_2 output is required?

In general, 4.6–10.3 lb of CO_2 per barrel (1.8–2.0 kg/hl) is required. An efficient and well-maintained system should be able to recover approximately 10.3 lb of CO_2 per barrel (2.0 kg/hl). Some loss of CO_2 will occur, because no recovery process is 100% efficient, but a brewery should be able to recover enough to meet the demands of its process (Kunze, 1996, pp. 393–394).

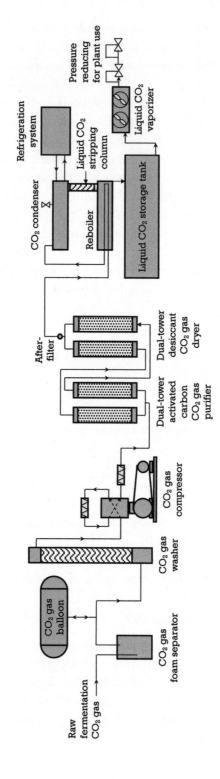

Figure 4.1. Purification and compression of carbon dioxide harvested from fermentation. (Courtesy of Haffmans B.V.)

14. What types of solid waste are generated, and what can be done with the waste streams?

a. Spent grains.   Next to water, grain is the raw material that a brewery consumes and disposes of in the largest amounts. Approximately 100 to 150 lb of wet spent grains is produced from every 100 lb of malt used. On average, wet spent grains consist of 70–80% water. An analysis of dried wet spent grains reported by Kunze (1996, p. 250) showed the following composition:

Protein	28 %
Fat	8.2
Nitrogen-free extract	41
Cellulose	17.5
Inorganic material	5.3

There are numerous uses for spent grain, from additives in baked goods to compost; spent grain from some Alaskan breweries is even being used as reindeer feed (Roberts, 2000). Cattle love the sweet grain, and farmers often mix it with silage to help prolong its storage time. The nutritional value of spent grain is much less than that of the same amount of dried barley, but the moisture makes it easily digestible by ruminants.

Mushroom growers also consider spent grain mixed with wood or grasses an excellent growing medium. A Japanese brewery has experimented with "gasifying" wet spent grain to create a gas fuel, which is used to run a fuel cell.

b. Grain chaff and malt dust.   Malt dust and chaff can be collected by dust control systems as elegant as vacuum-driven systems or as simple as a dust sock. Malt dust can be added to spent grain, and the chaff can be added to *kieselguhr* waste.

c. Spent yeast.   Yeast can be sold or given away as cattle food or even processed into vitamin supplements.

d. *Kieselguhr* slurry (DE).   Spent DE can be composted or used as a soil amendment or an ingredient in cement.

e. Cardboard.   Cardboard is easily recycled and can be baled and sold to recover some capital investment. It can also be used as worm food for composting. A baler used to recycle cardboard and stretch wrap is shown in *Figure 4.2,* and *Figure 4.3* shows 500-lb bales made from scrap cardboard and stretch wrap.

f. Plastic.   Plastic materials such as stretch wrap can be baled and sold for recycling.

g. Wood.   Wood can be recycled or used as fuel.

Figure 4.2. Cardboard and stretch wrap baler.

Figure 4.3. Compressed bales of scrap cardboard and stretch wrap, to be sold on the commodity market.

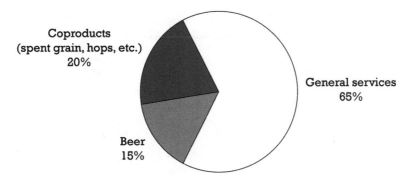

Figure 4.4. Water usage in a brewery producing 50,000 bbl per year. The water in beer accounts for only 15% of total water use. (Data from Watson, 1993)

15. What is wastewater?

Wastewater is possibly the most significant waste product of brewery operations. Although the amount varies widely, breweries use an average of seven barrels of water per barrel of beer produced (Watson, 1993). *Figure 4.4* shows water usage in a specialty brewery that produces 50,000 bbl per year. Though some of this water is boiled off or shipped out with the spent grain, up to 65% goes down the drain. Brewery wastewater is relatively biodegradable and nontoxic and generally does not negatively affect the local sewer system or publicly owned treatment works (POTW), which many smaller breweries rely on to process their effluent. Large slug loads of wort, beer, and/or chemicals, however, can have a negative impact even on large municipal sewer systems and can be disastrous for breweries discharging directly into waterways.

16. Why is wastewater a big issue for brewers?

Since brewing uses such large amounts of water, breweries are often some of the largest users of water in their communities. The character and strength of brewery effluent can put a heavy load on the POTW. Most municipalities levy expensive extra-strength sewer charges (ESSC) to encourage industries to reduce loads discharged into the sewer system. These charges can be substantial. *Table 4.1* shows the loading strengths of some common brewery effluent components, compared with allowable limits. ESSCs will continue to increase, providing strong incentives to install pretreatment systems, and increasing the return on investment in such systems.

Table 4.1. Loading strengths of common components of brewery effluent versus limits allowed by publicly owned treatment works (POTW)[a]

	Permitted by POTW	Trub	Spent yeast	Spent DE[b]	Beer
BOD[c] (mg/L)	300	118,000	110,000	300,000	81,300
TSS[d] (mg/L)	350	67,950	50,000	NA	0

[a] Source: City of Portland Environmental Services Laboratory, Portland, Oregon, May 1999.
[b] Diatomaceous earth.
[c] Biochemical oxygen demand.
[d] Total suspended solids.

17. What are the main components of brewery wastewater? How is the strength of wastewater measured, and what are the main chemical constituents?

The principal pollutants from brewery wastewater are

a. Biochemical oxygen demand. Biochemical oxygen demand (BOD) is the quantity of oxygen used by a mixed population of microorganisms in the aerobic oxidation of organic matter, notably soluble carbohydrates, in brewery effluent (Bitton, 1994, p. 139). The most common test for determining the strength of brewery wastewater involves incubation of a bacterial culture at 68°F (20°C) for 5 days; the oxygen demand measured under these conditions, expressed in milligrams per liter, is denoted BOD_{20}^5. The BOD of brewery waste varies widely among breweries and depends to a large extent on water usage and how much of the high-BOD load is treated or separated prior to discharge. Nutrients that contribute to BOD promote the growth of algae, resulting in a fouling of waterways. The main components of brewery BOD are wort and beer residues from the brewhouse, cellars, and packaging operations. Cleaning chemicals, such as nitric and phosphoric acids, are also major sources of nutrients. The macronutrients include nitrogen compounds (NH_3, ammonia; NO_2, nitrite; and NO_3, nitrate) and phosphorus compounds (PO_4, phosphate).

b. Chemical oxygen demand. Chemical oxygen demand (COD) is the amount of oxygen required to chemically oxidize the organic carbon completely to CO_2. The COD test can be completed in 2 hours rather than 5 days, so it is used for process control in wastewater treatment plants. COD test kits (*Figure 4.5*) contain lead and silver ions and must be disposed of as hazardous waste (Hach Company, 2002, pp. 742–743). COD is expressed as parts per million (mg/L).

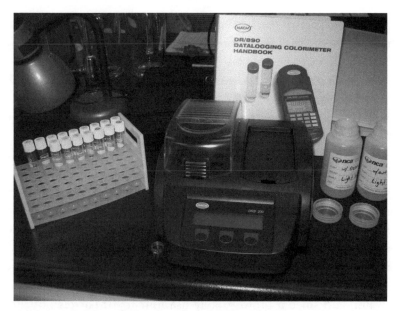

Figure 4.5. Chemical oxygen demand test equipment setup. Testing equipment consists of test tubes to hold samples and reagents, a heated test-tube block for chemical reaction, and either a colorimeter or spectrophotometer for taking wavelength readings at 620 nm. The test takes about 2–4 hours to react and then cool to room temperature.

c. Total suspended solids. Total suspended solids (TSS) are solids that do not dissolve into the effluent solution. The insoluble solids in brewery effluent can contribute to BOD. TSS testing is done by passing a presettled, measured sample through a 1.58-micron glass fiber filter and dividing the dried weight by the sample volume. TSS is expressed as parts per million (mg/L).

d. pH. Acidic waste has a pH less than 7, and caustic waste has a pH greater than 7, as measured with standard pH meters. Most underground municipal wastewater piping is concrete, which is highly sensitive to acidic waste. POTW plant bacteria are also sensitive to pH less than 6. The optimal pH for an aerobic wastewater treatment system is 7–7.5. Below pH 6, the growth of fungi can cause a bulking sludge (Bitton, 1994, p. 176). Even small pub breweries should consider neutralizing their wastewater before discharge.

18. What pretreatments are used for brewery wastewater?

There are several different levels of wastewater treatment possible, and the level at which it is treated depends greatly on where it is discharged and the size of the brewery operation. Brewery effluent is usually discharged into the POTW; some large plants discharge directly into waterways. The POTW usually dictates treatment standards through the issuance of industrial discharge permits. The treatments can be classified into two primary groups:

a. pH adjustment.   Federal law, 40 CFR Sec 403.5(b)(2), requires that the pH of the wastewater stream be adjusted to greater than 5.0 prior to discharge into the POTW. The upper range is set by the POTW and is usually less than pH 11.5. The allowable range varies from area to area and should be confirmed. Acids and bases are used to neutralize wastewater in batch or continuous-flow systems.

b. Effluent load reduction.   In most areas, the POTW assesses expensive surcharges to process wastewater with heavy BOD and TSS loads. In Portland, Oregon, the charges are $0.46 and $0.55 per pound, respectively. These ESSCs may add up to as much as $0.70 per barrel of wastewater, and since a brewery may use four to 10 barrels of water for each barrel of beer produced, the charges can be considerable. There are several strategies for reducing effluent loads.

19. What parameters must be considered when determining the need for wastewater treatment and design of a system?

a. Wastewater parameters

Average daily flow
Peak daily flow
Average BOD
Peak BOD
Average TSS
Peak TSS
Size distribution of suspended solids
Average temperature
pH range
Nutrient loads

b. Financial information

Municipal fees for constructing infrastructure to treat wastewater
Operational fees for wastewater treatment
Consultant costs
ESSCs

c. Treatment information

Municipal treatment capacity

20. What other factors should be considered?

a. Can the municipality handle the brewery's waste? Breweries located in small towns or resort areas may find that the local sewer plant does not have the capacity to process the high-strength wastewater that even a brew pub produces. Breweries in larger cities should also consult the POTW to determine limiting factors and special considerations that may affect them.

b. What are the capital and operational costs associated with treatment? Both the system equipment and its operations in terms of staffing and maintenance must be considered.

c. Are government incentive programs or grants available to help offset the capital investment? State and federal programs exist that offer significant tax incentives for companies installing waste systems. These incentives can make the difference in the number of years it takes for the project to return initial investment.

d. What guarantees can be secured from the system vendor? Guarantees on system performance as well as equipment function should extend from system start-up through an acceptable period to allow for adjustments and verifications.

21. What is the most basic treatment needed?

The most basic wastewater treatment required of almost every brewery is to adjust pH to the range stipulated by federal regulations and the POTW prior to discharge. Local authorities have no ability to waive these requirements.

22. What systems are used for pH adjustment?

There are two primary systems for pH adjustment:

a. Batch system. Small breweries and pub breweries can implement a simple one- or two-tank batch system with aboveground or belowground holding tanks or lined concrete vaults. The system requires a collection sump and pump for aboveground applications. A reliable pH probe and meter are required. All process wastewater should be collected in the holding tanks, and then the pH is adjusted by adding an acidifying agent, such as sulfuric acid or preferably CO_2 gas, or an alkalizing agent,

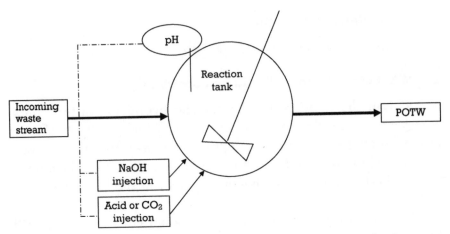

Figure 4.6. Single-tank system for wastewater pH adjustment in a batch process before discharge to the publicly owned treatment works (POTW). (Reprinted, by permission, from Ockert, 2002)

usually concentrated sodium hydroxide. When the pH of the wastewater in the tank reaches the required range, it is pumped out or diverted to the POTW. Regulatory agencies usually require a logbook or electronic data recorder to record the date, pH, and volumes discharged. *Figure 4.6* is a schematic of a simple single-tank batch system.

    b. Continuous system. Large plants discharging higher volumes than may be practical for a batch system but requiring pH adjustment may want to use a continuous system (*Figure 4.7*). A continuous system consists of a central collection vault or tank and up to two or three mixing and adjustment tanks, each outfitted with pH probes, mixers, chemical injectors, and sometimes aerators. As wastewater moves from tank to tank by continuous decant, the pH is monitored, and acidic or alkaline chemicals are injected as needed. By the time the waste stream has passed through the system, its pH is within the allowable range. Continuous systems usually record pH levels with data loggers for inspection purposes and also include magnetic-type flowmeters to measure the volume of wastewater sent to the POTW. Tanks and pumps must be sized for adequate residence time to allow for chemical reaction and mixing. *Figures 4.8* and *4.9* show a two-tank system used to adjust pH on a continuous-flow basis.

23. What strategies can reduce effluent load?

    a. Separation of materials with high effluent load. The most cost-effective method for significantly reducing effluent load is to avoid

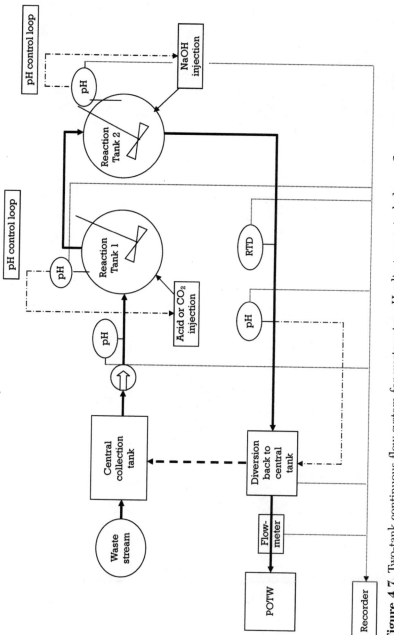

Figure 4.7. Two-tank continuous-flow system for wastewater pH adjustment, including a flowmeter and data recorder to record the pH and volume of wastewater discharged to the publicly owned treatment works (POTW); RTD, resistance temperature detector. (Reprinted, by permission, from Ockert, 2002)

Figure 4.8. Underground collection vault with manhole and self-priming centrifugal "trash" pump.

Figure 4.9. Two-tank pH adjustment system. The tank on the right takes in-feed from the collection vault. The pH of the water in this tank is lowered by the injection of CO_2 gas. The effluent decants through a flowmeter to the tank on the left, where low pH is adjusted by the addition of sodium hydroxide. The treated effluent is decanted to the publicly owned treatment works.

adding it to the wastewater stream in the first place. Unless designed into the plant, separation is not a convenient strategy, and in large plants it may not be practical, but for many small specialty and pub brewers, this strategy pays off quickly. The separation method requires a destination for the discharge outside the POTW. The discharge is commonly used for feeding animals or land fertilizer applications. The equipment necessary includes holding vessels or tanker trucks that can haul away the material, pumps, and dedicated piping or hoses for transfer. The materials with the highest BOD and TSS coming out of the plant are trub, spent yeast and tank bottoms, ullage from racking operations, and spent DE from filtration. DE can be bagged and disposed of in a landfill or used as a soil amendment. Spent yeast is very high in protein and B vitamins, and may be given to ruminant animals as a feeding supplement. *Table 4.2* gives the partial composition of dried brewer's yeast. Live yeast may harm ruminants if they are allowed to gorge, but when used to feed ruminants in measured amounts or mixed with a dry feed, live yeast can actually aid digestion (Bruning and Yokoyama, 1988). To allow animals to gorge freely on the material, the yeast should be killed before release by the brewery. Heating is the most common method of killing yeast. The stirred mixture can be brought up to 130–140°F (55–60°C) and held for 12 hours for a complete kill. All isolated liquid materials are pumped to a central tank or tanker truck and hauled off site for disposal as land fertilizer, distillation, or animal feed. *Table 4.3* shows some common uses for brewing coproducts.

b. Aerobic systems. Aerobic systems will be described in more detail, but essentially they involve methods of removing TSS and hence some BOD through mechanical aeration and flocculation (dissolved air flotation, or DAF), which may be coupled with aerobic biological digestion using aerated microbial reactor beds. High reductions of BOD and

Table 4.2. Partial composition of dried, unfortified brewer's yeast

Major component	Concentration (g/100 g)	Vitamin	Concentration (mg/100 g)
Protein	50	Niacin	50
Carbohydrate	42	Thiamin	15
Ash	7	Pantothenate	10
Fat	6	Riboflavin	7
Moisture	5	Folic acid	4
		Pyridoxine	3
		Biotin	0.2

[a] Reprinted, by permission, from Lewis and Young (2001), p. 159.

Table 4.3. Off-site disposal options for brewery coproducts[a]

Coproduct	Source	Attributes	Uses
Spent grain	Lauter tun	High carbohydrate, protein	Cattle feed
Sweet water	Lauter tun	High carbohydrate	Animal feed
Spent hops	Brew kettle	High carbohydrates	Animal feed, soil amendment
Trub	Whirlpool tank	High carbohydrate	Cattle feed
Spent yeast	Tank bottoms	High protein	Animal feed, distillation
Spent DE[b]	Filtration	Porous silica	Soil amendment
Ullage	Racker	Ethanol	Distillation

[a] Reprinted, by permission, from Ockert, 2002.
[b] Diatomaceous earth.

TSS can be realized, and capital costs are reasonable, given the high sewer surcharges that must otherwise be paid, but the system produces large amounts of sludge that must be disposed of and does not yield any usable coproduct such as methane.

c. Anaerobic digestion systems.   Anaerobic systems are efficient in reducing BOD and TSS and do not generate large amounts of sludge. Many even produce usable methane gas as a by-product. However, anaerobic systems are delicate and require more capital and expertise than either of the two other methods, and the operational costs of anaerobic systems are higher.

24. What are the levels of wastewater treatment?

There are three levels of treatment:

a. Removal of solids.   Typical solids that need to be removed from brewery waste are diatomaceous earth, glass, bottle caps, plastic, and spent grain—basically, anything that can get into the drain. These materials are removed from wastewater by the use of screens, grit chambers, and settling ponds. It is a good idea to install drain screens in floor drains to catch things such as clamp gaskets that can clog the system and possibly damage pumps downstream.

b. Biological treatment and settling.   The biological processes in wastewater treatment can be either aerobic or anaerobic. During this stage, pH is adjusted, and BOD, COD, and TSS levels are reduced.

c. Advanced waste treatment and water reuse.   Wastewater is further treated to remove or destroy pathogens. Processes used to disinfect wastewater include UV filtration, ultrafiltration, and chemical treatment (Davis and Cornwell, 1991, p. 333). With proper treatment, water may be reused several times within the plant.

25. How does anaerobic digestion work, and why is it appropriate for brewery wastewater?

Anaerobic digestion works well for industrial wastewater that has a high organic load. Most brewery wastewater is considered high strength (COD > 1,000 mg/L). Aerobic digestion is better suited to low-strength wastewater (COD < 1,000 mg/L).

Anaerobic digestion is a two-stage biological process. The first stage consists of acidification performed by facultative bacteria, which degrade organic matter into gases, such as CO_2, H_2S, and methane, and organic acids. The second stage is performed by strict anaerobic bacteria, which degrade the organic acids produced in the first stage to CO_2, methane, and H_2S. Facultative and anaerobic bacteria grow under different conditions. The acidifiers can tolerate very low pH levels, grow rapidly, and respond well to varying loads. In contrast, the methanogenic bacteria in the second stage require a pH range of 6.8–7.4, are highly sensitive to load changes, and grow very slowly. Acidifiers require a temperature of 95–102°F (35–39°C) while methanogens function best at 95°F (35°C). In this configuration, the acidifying bacteria protect the methane-producing bacteria and provide a steady stream of easily digestible waste.

26. What types of anaerobic digesters are available?

Two types of anaerobic digesters are described below. However, there are many variations on these designs.

a. Upflow anaerobic sludge blanket. The upflow anaerobic sludge blanket digester has been around since the beginning of the twentieth century. It was first used in the Netherlands for treating industrial wastewater from the food industry (Bitton, 1994, p. 241). The reactor consists of three layers: a bottom layer of packed sludge, a sludge blanket, and a liquid upper layer. Wastewater flows up from the bottom through the sludge layers, and settling screens separate the sludge and allow the water and gas to flow out the top. This type of reactor has a compact design and is capable of handling high COD loads (10–15 kg of $COD/m^3/day$) (Biothane Corporation website, 2005).

b. Fluidized bed reactor. During the 1970s, fluidized bed reactors were put into use. Wastewater flows in through the bottom of the reactor and up through a sand bed. The sand provides a growth area for the biofilm. The wastewater must be circulated through the bed at a flow rate high enough to create a fluidized bed. The advantages of a fluidized bed design include excellent contact with microorganisms and high bio-mass concentrations, which translate into reduced reactor volumes. Suc-cessful treatment of wastewater with low COD (<1,000 mg/L) at low operating temperatures and short retention times (<6 hours) are possible with this design (Bitton, 1994, p. 243).

27. What are the pros and cons of anaerobic wastewater treatment?

Brewery wastewater is easily treated. The high carbohydrate and pro-tein loads contained in brewery waste are easily digested by microbial ac-tivity. The benefits of anaerobic digestion include

a. Creation of biogas. Anaerobic bacteria produce biogas that is 80–90% methane. This gas contains 9,000 kcal/m^3 and is easily burned in natural gas equipment with some minor modifications. Biogas contains H$_2$S, which is very corrosive and has to be removed if the gas is to be used as an energy source. The concentration of H$_2$S depends on the concentra-tion of sulfur in the wastewater being treated.

b. Less sludge production. Unlike aerobic digestion, anaerobic digestion does not produce a bacterial biomass. Thus, there is significantly less sludge to deal with than with aerobic digestion.

c. Energy reduction. The energy required for wastewater treat-ment is reduced since no aeration is required.

d. Suitability for high-load effluents. Anaerobic processes are suitable for high-strength industrial waste such as brewery waste and can handle high loading rates.

Some of the disadvantages include

a. Temperature sensitivity. The microbes require a temperature of 95°F (35°C).

b. pH sensitivity. The optimal pH is 6.8–7.4. If the pH is below 6, anaerobic digestion can stop completely.

c. Sensitivity to toxins. Some cleaning line lubrication chemicals are incompatible with the microbes that perform anaerobic digestion.

d. Time. A lengthy start-up process is required.

e. Odor. The process needs to be well sealed from the atmos-phere, and waste gases need to be treated for odor.

f. Sludge containment. The sludge is hard to contain in the re-actor. Unlike aerobic sludge, which settles well (provided everything is working correctly), anaerobic sludge tends to be less dense and has en-trained gas, causing it to float.

g. Continuous flow required.   The process is not suited to large variations in flow.

28. How does aerobic digestion work?

Aerobic systems take advantage of both mechanical and biological methods of reducing wastewater BOD and TSS. Compact systems are available that can combine the functions of pH adjustment, suspended solids flocculation. Microbial digestion requires relatively large vessels. Typically, a system consists of the following:

a. Underground vessel or vault serving as a central sump for drains from the process areas and floor drains

b. Balance tank to reduce the effects of surges in wastewater flow (this stage may also incorporate screening to remove large solids from the system)

c. pH adjustment tank or tanks to bring pH within the range required by the coagulants and flocculants used and within the range allowed by the POTW

d. Bioreactor vessels with heavy aeration to digest dissolved solids.

e. Chemical injection of coagulants and flocculants, either in-line or in reaction vessels

f. Dissolved air flotation (DAF) system with aeration to form flocs from suspended solids and skimming to remove the material to a sludge-holding vessel

Systems like the one described below, especially in conjunction with a high BOD-TSS load separation program, can significantly reduce the BOD in brewery wastewater.

29. How does the DAF system work?

The DAF system is designed to make very small particles of insoluble suspended solids into larger ones and then to remove these large particles from the waste stream by flotation and skimming. Typically, the process starts with removal of large, settleable solids followed by adjustment of the wastewater pH to 6–9. The effluent then enters a mixed coagulent chamber, where coagulant chemicals are injected to attract fine, charged particles, forming small "pin flocs." The stream then goes to a mixed flocculation chamber, where a long-chain "sticky" polymer flocculant of speci-

Figure 4.10. Sludge is skimmed off at the top of the dissolved air flotation unit. The sludge is formed by the interaction of effluent insoluble solids with injected coagulant and flocculent chemicals. The precipitated sludge is then skimmed off mechanically and pumped away to a holding tank for disposal. (Courtesy of World Water Works)

fied charge (anionic or cationic) attracts and precipitates the fine pin flocs into large, easily visible flocs.

The effluent stream is then blended with supersaturated aerated water. The saturated air forms fine bubbles, attracting and floating the large flocs to the surface to be removed by skimmer machines. The skimmed material goes to a sludge tank for disposal, and the treated water flows by gravity to the next stage (*Figure 4.10*).

Air saturation can be done with compressed air in a separate high-pressure saturation tank, although designs for aspirated air systems exist. *Figure 4.11* shows a DAF system process detail for an aspirated air system. DAF systems are widely available in several designs and can be made of painted mild steel, stainless steel, and polyethylene. These systems are promising for small breweries with limited space. *Figure 4.12* shows a DAF unit capable of processing 60 gallons per minute in a 60-ft^2 footprint.

30. How effective is the DAF system alone?

Flocculation and removal of suspended solids in the DAF system can significantly reduce the wastewater load. *Figure 4.13* shows virtually

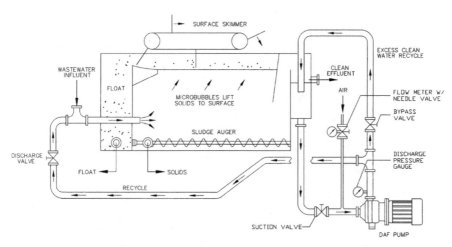

Figure 4.11. Dissolved air flotation system, in which an aeration pump is used to form microbubbles that carry flocculated suspended solids to the surface, where they are skimmed off and removed. (Courtesy of PanAmerican Environmental, Inc.)

Figure 4.12. Dissolved air flotation (DAF) unit capable of processing 60 gallons per minute of wastewater. Larger DAF units are commonly used in municipal sewer plants, pulp and paper operations, and large food-manufacturing plants processing thousands of gallons per hour. (Courtesy of World Water Works)

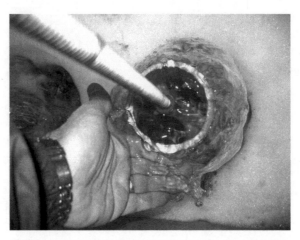

Figure 4.13. Treated effluent exiting the dissolved air flotation (DAF) weir is almost completely free of insoluble solids. The final biochemical oxygen demand of the effluent can be reduced across the DAF as solids that contribute to organic loads are removed. (Courtesy of World Water Works)

solids-free effluent coming off a DAF that is processing 900-ppm TSS influent. The system should practically eliminate TSS and, depending on the characteristics of the effluent, may significantly reduce the BOD value by removing insoluble BOD materials in the suspended solids. The wastewater should be chemically tested in advance to estimate the expected reductions, but it may be possible to significantly reduce the ESSCs levied by the POTW with a system ending at the DAF system and without further aerobic digestion. DAF does not remove total dissolved solids (TDS), such as sugars, from the effluent. The removal of TDS requires further aerobic digestion. *Table 4.4* shows DAF trials at a 50,000-barrel-per-year brewery. Note the variability in COD loads and reductions.

31. How is the sludge disposed of?

The sludge generated by the DAF system may be dewatered and disposed of in a landfill, used as a soil amendment, or, depending on its content, used as animal feed.

32. What aerobic treatments are available?

Several methods are used to reduce BOD using aerobic microbes. The most common methods in industrial applications are activated sludge systems, and the most common activated sludge treatment is the sequen-

Table 4.4. Changes in chemical oxygen demand (COD, mg/L) levels of brewery wastewater after treatment through a dissolved air floatation (DAF) system

Sample	Pretreatment (mg/L)	Post DAF (mg/L)	COD reduction (mg/L)	Removal (%)
1	5,690	4,270	1,420	25.0
2	2,160	1,910	250	11.6
3	2,390	2,052	338	14.1
4	4,323	3,632	691	16.0
5	2,350	1,980	370	15.7
6	3,700	1,650	2,050	55.4
7	2,750	1,880	870	31.6
8	3,980	1,710	2,270	57.0
9	5,910	3,490	2,420	40.9
10	5,220	3,340	1,880	36.0
11	6,660	4,302	2,358	35.4
12	1,870	1,692	178	9.5
13	5,320	3,248	2,072	38.9
14	3,900	3,300	600	15.4
15	3,740	3,360	380	10.2
16	1,910	1,576	334	17.5
17	1,870	1,566	304	16.3
Average	3,750	2,645	1,105	26
Std. Dev.	1,576	996	871	15

[a] Source: BridgePort Brewing Company (2004).

tial batch reactor (SBR). The SBR uses at least two vessels, which are filled and processed sequentially in batches. The effluent is mixed and aerated along with living microorganisms (active sludge). The microorganisms oxidize and digest the nutrients in the effluent, creating energy and biomass. The vessel goes through a program of mixing, reacting, settling, and decanting in batches. Portions of the generated sludge are seeded into each new batch, and the excess is dewatered and disposed of normally by landfill.

Moving bed biofilm reactor (MBBR) systems use plastic media in the holding vessels. The media come in different shapes but essentially consist of small perforated pieces of plastic, on which the microbes grow and cover every surface. This substantially increases the surface area of microbial contact in the system. The media are mixed or moved continuously in the effluent by forced air currents through diffusers at the bottom of the vessel, which creates constant contact with the effluent material. The increase in the biofilm area per unit volume, along with continuous mixing of the biofilm area with the effluent, allows both a smaller footprint and continuous operation, which differentiate it from the SBR. As the biofilm sloughs off, suspended biomass is removed from the outgoing effluent either by a settling tank or DAF.

Regardless of the system used, the aerobic digestion system's retention time is based on a function of BOD content and microbe population. The relatively long residence time for aerobic digestion as opposed to anaerobic digestion normally translates to larger holding vessels and hence larger footprints. Residence times ranging from 8 to 12 hours or even longer are necessary for the process to reduce the BOD loads by 90%. Continuous aeration is supplied by blowers to obtain 2–4 ppm of dissolved oxygen. Aeration is accomplished using various mechanical devices or by diffusers. The reaction consumes 0.6–0.8 lb of oxygen per pound of COD supplied. In addition, 1 lb of COD yields 0.5–0.8 lb of sludge in the form of biomass (Crites and Tchobanoglous, 1998, p. 458). This biomass must be removed from the system and disposed of either as landfill or fertilizer.

The bacteria in aerobic systems are generally more tolerant to pH and temperature swings than anaerobic bacteria are. The pH of the system should range from 7.0 to 7.5. Aerobic bacteria are less sensitive to alkaline pH than to acidic pH, and systems going below pH 6 may encounter problems (Liu and Liptak, 1999, p. 183).

33. What are the pros and cons of aerobic wastewater treatment?

The benefits of aerobic DAF and digestion include

a. Low capital costs.   Because the aerobic process does not require the mechanization and gas collection equipment that the anaerobic process needs, DAF and bioreacting systems are less expensive than anaerobic systems.

b. Ease of operation.   These systems do not require complicated automation and controls, and aerobic microbes are able to tolerate greater fluctuations in pH, flow, and temperatures than anaerobic microbes.

c. Less odor.   The aerobic process does not produce H_2S or methane gases, which are highly odiferous, unpleasant, and problematic in an urban environment.

The disadvantages are

a. High operational costs.   DAF costs are tied mostly to the chemicals needed to form the sludge and the electrical energy needed to operate the pumps and the mechanical and aeration equipment. Bioreactors use electrical energy for blowers.

b. Sludge. Large amounts of biomass sludge are generated, requiring some method of disposal.

c. Less suitability for high-load wastewater. Aerobic DAF systems work best in conjunction with a program of separating and removing materials that create high BOD from the waste stream. Higher loads require more residence time in the bioreactor. (A DAF unit and bioreactor may reduce BOD and TSS averaging 2,500 and 900 ppm, respectively, to as little as 25 and 10 ppm.)

d. High space requirements. The long residence times for wastewater in aerobic digesters require large holding vessels and footprints. This may pose a problem for breweries located in tight urban environments or lacking sufficient outdoor space.

REFERENCES

Biothane Corporation. 2005. http://www.biothane.com/default.aspx?sel=3

Bitton, G. 1994. *Wastewater Microbiology.* Wiley-Liss, New York.

Bruning, C. L., and Yokoyama, M. T. 1988. Characteristics of live and killed brewer's yeast slurries and intoxication by intraruminal administration to cattle. *Journal of Animal Science* 66:585–591.

Crites, R., and Tchobanoglous, G. 1998. *Small and Decentralized Wastewater Systems.* McGraw-Hill, New York.

Davis, M. L., and Cornwell, D. 1991. *Introduction to Environmental Engineering.* 2d ed. McGraw-Hill, New York.

Environmental Protection Agency. 2002. A comprehensive analysis of biodiesel impacts on exhaust emissions. EPA420-P-02-001. EPA, Washington, D.C.

Hach Company. 2002. *Water Treatment Analysis Handbook.* 4th ed. Hach, Loveland, Colo.

Heyse, K.-U., Hiller, N., and Beer, R. 1996. Environmental protection in the brewery. *Technical Quarterly of the Master Brewers Association of the Americas* 33:246–254.

Kunze, W. 1996. *Technology Brewing and Malting.* International ed. Versuchs- und Lehranstalt für Brauerei, Berlin.

Lewis, M. J., and Young, T. W. 2001. *Brewing.* Aspen Publishers, Gaithersburg, Md.

Liu, D. H. F., and Liptak, B. G., eds. 1999. *Wastewater Treatment.* CRC Press, Boca Raton, Fla.

Ockert, K. 2002. Practical wastewater pretreatment strategies for small breweries. *Technical Quarterly of the Master Brewers Association of the Americas* 39:39–46.

Roberts, J. 2000. Rising from the kettle: There's life in that barley yet. Anchorage Press. http://www.anchorage press.com/archives/document01cf.html

Union Engineering. 2005. http://www.union.dk/page.php?emne_id=437

Watson, C. 1993. Wastewater minimisation and effluent disposal at a brewery. *Technical Quarterly of the Master Brewers Association of the Americas* 30:114–117.

SUGGESTION FOR FURTHER READING

Kinton, K. 1999. Environmental issues affecting brewery operations. Pages 611–645 in: *The Practical Brewer: A Manual for the Brewing Industry.* 3d ed. J. T. McCabe, ed. Master Brewers Association of the Americas, Wauwatosa, Wisc.

CHAPTER 5

Safety in the Brewery

Jim Kelter

Full Sail Brewing Company

1. What is the importance of safety in the brewing process?

Brewing beers and ales involves a number of processes that require a broad array of mechanical equipment and incorporate a variety of materials. Injury, illness, and even death can result if machines are not operated properly and materials are not handled properly. The health and well-being of workers are of critical importance, as it is in any workplace. To ensure safety in the brewery, it is important that the brewer be aware of potential hazards. Safety can be achieved by understanding the materials and equipment used in the process and training employees in their proper use and their potential hazards.

2. What potential hazards exist in the brewery?

Potential hazards can be classified as mechanical, chemical, environmental, and ergonomic.

a. Mechanical hazards. Any hazard related to the operation of mechanical equipment in the brewhouse, such as pumps, mills, packaging equipment, and conveyors, is a mechanical hazard. Any equipment used to facilitate the mechanical transfer and handling of material, be it wort, beer, grain, or glass, is also included. Lockout-tagout programs are intended to address these hazards.

b. Chemical hazards. Nearly all chemicals pose a potential hazard if not used or handled properly. Various chemicals are used for cleaning and sanitizing the brewhouse, cellars, and packaging areas. Compressed gases, such as oxygen, acetylene, and carbon dioxide (CO_2), are also commonly used, both in production and for maintenance purposes. A

159

thorough hazard communication plan related to chemical safety should be prepared.

    c. Environmental hazards.   Environmental hazards range from inadequate workplace lighting and clutter on the floors, which impede safe movement, to elevated levels of noise in the brewing and production areas that can contribute to permanent hearing loss. Airborne particulates, such as malt dust, diatomaceous earth, and other powdered or dusty compounds, can pose respiratory hazards. Confined space hazards, such as CO_2 in empty fermentation vessels, warrant implementation of a confined space protocol and training to ensure worker safety.

    d. Ergonomic hazards.   Some operations can inflict bodily stresses and strains. Back strain and injury can result from handling heavy or bulky items, such as bags of malt or bales of hops. Repetitive motion injuries in a production environment are also common. Such injuries can be minimized or eliminated with ergonomic engineering and design.

3. Who is responsible for safety in the brewery?

    The employer bears the ultimate responsibility for ensuring that all employees are aware of the hazards they may face in the workplace. All U.S. employers must post a notice informing employees of their rights under the Occupational Safety and Health Act and standards set by the Occupational Safety and Health Administration (OSHA). Creating a safe workplace, however, requires cooperation between employer and employees. Workers who are informed of their rights to a safe workplace and are informed of the risks they may face are more likely to contribute to workplace safety by identifying hazards and proposing solutions. This enhances the safety of workers and helps to reduce hours lost because of injury. An additional benefit of a safely run plant is reduced workers' compensation insurance premiums.

4. How can employees be informed of safety issues?

    Effective means of communicating with employees include publication of the company safety policy, training employees in the company safety policy, posting notices, and the formation of a safety committee as a forum for discussion of safety with employees. Open discussion of safety and visual reminders of safety policy foster a safety-focused culture in the workplace.

5. What is a safety committee?

A safety committee is a means of bringing brewery management and workers together in a cooperative effort to promote safety and health in the workplace. The committee acts in an advisory capacity by assessing workplace safety and recommending safety policy and procedures to the employer. The committee should include a cross section of employees from various departments as well as a management representative. Membership should rotate, to encourage the participation of all employees. A safety committee can be a valuable tool in helping promote safety consciousness. Safety committees are also required by OSHA to conduct quarterly plant walkthroughs and identify potential safety hazards that are then addressed by the company.

6. What programs and policies are needed to operate a plant safely?

a. Lockout-tagout program
b. Hazard communications program
c. Confined space protocol
d. Emergency action plan
e. General plant safety protocols
f. Back safety
g. Hearing conservation
h. Personal protection equipment
i. Forklift safety and certification
j. Fire safety
k. Facility-specific hazardous systems policy and training

Some policies and programs commonly used to build a plant safety program are shown in *Table 5.1.*

7. What is a lockout-tagout program?

Workers performing maintenance or service on machinery are exposed to the risk of injury resulting from the release of stored energy or the inadvertent or unexpected activation of equipment. Lockout-tagout is the process whereby workers release this stored energy and isolate the equipment being serviced from its energy source to eliminate the potential hazard. A lockout-tagout program should include the following:

a. Definitions of program policy
b. Key points to the proper lockout

Table 5.1. Programs and policies for plant safety

Program or policy	Goal	Implementation
Lockout-tagout program	Reduce chance of injury caused by unexpected machinery starts	Various devices, locks, and tags to prevent accidental restarts
Hazard communication plan	Reduce injury caused by accidental exposure to chemicals	Staff training, container labeling, and material safety data sheets
Confined space entry	Eliminate injury caused by hazardous conditions in confined spaces where rescue is difficult	Permit procedure, ventilation equipment, oxygen meters, and lockouts
Emergency action plan	Plan for emergency evacuation and accounting of personnel	Site maps, escape routes, emergency lighting, and communications
Hearing conservation plan	Monitor and respond to conditions that can cause hearing damage	Hearing protection equipment and yearly testing
Personal protection equipment	Protect eyes, ears, feet, and hands	Equipment including gloves, hearing protection, eye protection, and approved footwear
General plant safety policy	Reduce or eliminate common and avoidable accidents	Training, policy, and procedures to eliminate common hazards
Back safety	Eliminate or reduce back strain and injury	Training in proper lifting technique, establish limits, engineering solutions
Forklift certification	Eliminate accidents related to lack of training in the operation of forklift trucks	OSHA-required program of lecture and practical training and testing
Fire safety	Reduce fire risk	Fire prevention training, fire detection and fire suppression equipment
Facility-specific policies	Address situations unique to each facility	Training, equipment, and procedures crafted for each situation

    c. Lockout-tagout procedures
    d. Lockout equipment and specifications for use
    e. Employee training and orientation

8. How does a lockout-tagout program work?

A lockout-tagout program mandates that all employees authorized to perform maintenance or to service equipment have the knowledge and equipment necessary to effect a complete shutdown and isolation of the equipment from potentially hazardous energy sources. Written documentation should be prepared for each machine. Operators and non-maintenance personnel must also be familiar with lockout-tagout procedures.

Persons authorized to work on equipment in which they are vulnerable to the effects of an unexpected start-up must follow these basic steps:

a. Determine the types of energy used in the operation of the equipment and the hazards posed by that energy. For example, some equipment may require both electrical and pneumatic or hydraulic power for operation. Other types of energy include steam and hot water. Any one of these, if not controlled, could cause injury.

b. Determine the means of controlling the energy used in the operation of the equipment (electrical breakers, isolation valves, bleed valves, etc.).

c. Notify affected workers of the shutdown.

d. Systematically shut down *all* sources of energy, and verify that the equipment is completely isolated.

e. Secure all controls by locking them out. Lockout devices must be able to hold energy sources in a neutral or off position. Various devices that enable a worker to lock all types of electrical switches and breakers and plumbing and air valves are available from safety equipment vendors. Once a control is locked out, a tag is affixed to the lockout device, indicating that it has been secured and identifying the person who locked it out.

f. Test all controls to verify that stored or residual energy has been disconnected or relieved before the work begins.

g. Reset the devices when the work is finished. Only the person performing the lockout may carry the lockout key and reset the device. If more than one worker is performing the task, each one should affix a lock and an identifying tag to the device or devices being locked out. This procedure ensures the safety of all workers involved in the repair.

h. Notify affected workers when the lockout has been released.

Lockout devices must be designed to prevent removal other than by a key. Each device must be uniquely keyed and must singularly identify the user. Tagout devices must identify the user and must be able to withstand the environmental extremes common in breweries (e.g., excessive wetness and exposure to chemicals).

All workers must be trained in a lockout-tagout program. Training should be provided regularly and updated as needed to include new

Figure 5.1. Electrical disconnect switch padlocked and tagged. (Courtesy of Full Sail Brewing Company)

equipment or modifications to the facility. Persons authorized to perform maintenance or repair equipment must be identified. They must be trained in energy control procedures for equipment in their area of responsibility and provided with devices to effectively lock out the equipment.

9. Can equipment be designed to facilitate a lockout-tagout program?

Keeping safety in mind when specifying new equipment and installations makes lockout-tagout procedures much easier to perform. Most production equipment is now available with lockout-friendly features. Power panel disconnects usually have switches that can be padlocked (*Figure 5.1*), and valves with handles having a lockout feature are available. When safety features are designed into the equipment, trained employees are more likely to perform these critical functions.

10. What is a hazard communications program?

In all workplaces where employees are exposed to hazardous chemicals, the OSHA Hazard Communication Standard (HSC) requires implementation of a program whereby all employees are informed of the hazardous nature of the chemicals with which they are working. Employers must prepare a written plan, known as a hazard communications program, describing how this standard is implemented in their facility.

11. What does a hazard communications program include?

a. List of hazardous materials on-site. The workplace should be surveyed to compile a list of all potentially hazardous materials used and stored on the premises. The Material Safety Data Sheet (MSDS) for each item listed in the inventory should be available.

b. MSDS records. A system should be implemented for filing MSDSs for hazardous materials used in the workplace. These records must be readily available to employees for periodic review and must be maintained to ensure that they are up to date. Suppliers should provide the MSDS for each product. MSDSs for many products are available from the Internet sites of their manufacturers. Many breweries keep MSDSs in binders at different locations around the plant, for chemicals used in those areas (*Figure 5.2*).

c. Container labeling. Persons responsible for maintaining chemical inventories must ensure that all material received is clearly labeled with the manufacturer's name and address, container content, and appropriate hazard warning.

d. Employee training. All employees must receive training that includes a review of chemicals used in the workplace, health risks associated with them, recommended procedures for safely using and handling them, personal protective equipment, and emergency procedures to follow in the event of an accident. This training should be provided as orientation for new employees and required of all employees annually. Chemical suppliers can often provide training.

e. List of nonroutine tasks. Tasks that are not performed regularly are listed and defined, giving detailed information on hazardous materials that are present and risks of exposure to them.

f. Piping labels. All piping in the plant must be clearly labeled to state the material contained in the pipe. Piping that contains materials such as steam, hot water, compressed air, and chemicals must be labeled

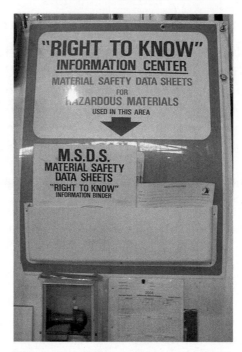

Figure 5.2. Material Safety Data Sheets posted in an accessible area of the plant. (Courtesy of Full Sail Brewing Company)

Figure 5.3. Clearly labeled water pipes and plant utility pipes. (Courtesy of BridgePort Brewing Company)

with easy-to-read, moisture-resistant tape (*Figure* 5.3). Standards for color-coding these labels have been established.

g. Considerations for outside contractors. Outside contractors performing work on the premises must be informed of the presence of chemicals stored at the job site and the hazards associated with them. The MSDS for any hazardous material must be made available to the contractor's employees. If a contractor brings a hazardous material on the premises, the employer must obtain its MSDS.

12. What potential hazards are related to the use of chemicals commonly found in the brewery?

As in any food-manufacturing facility, clean and sanitary conditions are critical in the brewery. Achieving the desired level of hygiene is not possible without the use of chemicals, and therefore caustics and acids are commonly present in the brewery. As with all chemicals, there are some risks inherent with their use.

a. Alkaline detergents, such as cleaning compounds containing sodium hydroxide (NaOH), are typically used in large volumes in most brewing, cellar, and packaging operations. NaOH is highly corrosive. Chemical burns are the most common injury related to the use of alkaline detergents. Depending upon the level of exposure, injuries can range from moderate irritation to severe (even permanent) damage to the skin or eyes. The severity of the injury increases with the concentration of the solution. Personal protective equipment is required when caustic chemicals are handled.

b. Acid detergents and sanitizers are frequently used in cleaning and sanitizing. Hydrochloric, nitric, and phosphoric acids can burn skin and eye tissue. The severity of injury from exposure increases with the concentration of the solution. Personal protective equipment must be worn when any acid is handled.

c. Sodium hypochlorite (chlorine bleach) is used for cleaning and sanitation in some brewhouses. It is a strong oxidizing agent and can be highly reactive with incompatible chemicals. Mixing sodium hypochlorite with an acid produces toxic chlorine gas, which can quickly fill an enclosed space and cause permanent lung damage and possibly death. Engineering controls, such as ventilation, should be used when large volumes of sodium hypochlorite are handled, and personal protective equipment is essential.

d. Compressed or cylinder gases are commonly used in brewing and packaging operations. Oxygen, acetylene, and liquefied petroleum

Figure 5.4. Secondary chemical container. Note closure and tag. (Courtesy of BridgePort Brewing Company)

(LP) gases are all highly flammable and present a significant potential for fire or explosion. This danger can be reduced through proper storage and handling. All gases such as these should be kept away from flames, sparks, and other ignition sources. Compressed oxygen should never be stored around other flammable gases. All equipment associated with the use of these gases must be properly maintained. All cylinders should be kept upright and chained to a secure object or wall.

13. What are some guidelines for safe handling of chemicals?

a. Chemicals should be stored in properly labeled containers (*Figure 5.4*). Buckets and transfer totes should also be properly labeled and should have caps to secure their contents and prevent spills.

b. Employees must be familiar with the chemicals in use and be trained in proper use and handling techniques. Many chemical suppliers offer seminars on the proper handling of chemicals.

c. Personal protective equipment, including chemical-resistant gloves and safety glasses, goggles, or face shield, must always be worn when chemicals are handled.

d. When a chemical is mixed with water, the chemical is *always* added to the water, to minimize the risk of splashing caused by a chemical reaction. Water is never added to the chemical.

e. Chlorine should never be mixed with any acid, because a potentially deadly chlorine gas may form. Acid and chlorine solutions should be kept separate in storage.

f. Oxygen should never be stored with flammable gases, such as LP. Cylinder gases must be secured to prevent tipping. Cylinders for portable units should be contained within a carrier or cart designed for that purpose. All compressed gas cylinders should be properly secured, both in storage and during transfer within the brewhouse.

g. Eyewash stations and showers should be installed near areas where chemicals are used or stored. The area around these stations must be left unimpeded for ready access in the event of an emergency.

h. MSDSs must be available to all employees, and the employees must be familiar with them.

14. What is an MSDS?

A Material Safety Data Sheet (MSDS) is a document providing assessments of the physical and health hazards of a product, prepared by the manufacturer or distributor of the product as required by OSHA. Users of hazardous materials are required to make these sheets accessible to employees and should ensure that the employees understand the information contained in them.

15. Why is the MSDS important?

The MSDS provides specific information that can help to prevent injuries to users. In addition to product identification, the MSDS gives a description of the chemical composition of the product and pertinent physical data, such as boiling point, melting point, vapor pressure and density, physical appearance, and viscosity. Data on fire and explosion hazards, reactivity, and health hazards are included, with recommendations for personal protection and emergency and first-aid procedures. There is an MSDS for each of numerous materials present in the brewery, from malt dust to filter sheets. Given the array of hazardous materials commonly used in the brewery, the MSDS is an important tool for understanding and assessing potential hazards and enhancing safety in the workplace. The MSDS can also be of great help to emergency care providers in treating people exposed to hazardous materials, by providing precise details on their chemical components.

16. What is confined space entry?

CO_2 gas is commonly present in brewing and packaging operations. It is a natural by-product of fermentation and is used in cellar and packaging operations. It is a colorless, odorless gas that is heavier than air. A high volume of CO_2 in an inadequately ventilated environment can cause suffocation. Fatalities have been documented when workers entered tanks for cleaning that were not properly ventilated. Clean-in-place (CIP) systems in brewing vessels and nonmanual yeast-harvesting methods have largely eliminated the need for workers to routinely enter beer tanks. However, workers still occasionally enter tanks to perform maintenance operations or carry out inspections. Brewers should have a confined space program for tanks requiring entry. This program must provide adequate safeguards against a hazardous atmosphere inside the tanks and protection from mechanical hazards, such as mixing arms and rake assemblies.

In general, a confined space is an enclosed or partially enclosed area that is not intended for continuous occupancy. It must be large enough for a worker to enter to perform work, but it has restricted means of entry or exit that may complicate rescue or emergency services. Brew vessels, malt bins, fermenters, and other enclosed vessels that periodically require entrance for maintenance, cleaning, or inspection fall under this definition. It is important that a confined space policy be formulated and that all employees be trained in confined space procedure. Confined space entry protocol should include the following:

a. **Atmosphere assessment.** Before a worker enters a fermenter or other beer tank, the atmosphere within the confined space must be assessed to determine whether it is conducive to safe exposure. This is a critical first step. Gas detectors are available that give a quick oxygen measurement to ensure a safe environment for tank entry (*Figure 5.5*). Any space containing an atmosphere of less than 19.5% oxygen is considered oxygen-deficient and should not be entered.

b. **Ventilation.** Where a hazardous atmosphere is present, a mechanical ventilation system must be used or air circulation must be increased to reduce harmful concentrations of hazardous gases to safe

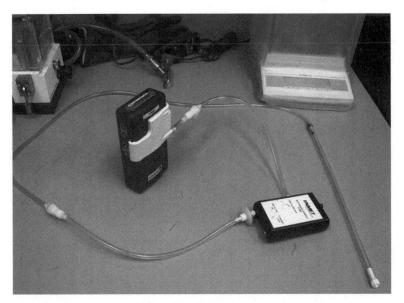

Figure 5.5. Air-testing meter for checking the oxygen level in a confined space before entry. (Courtesy of Full Sail Brewing Company)

levels. A small, portable blower (*Figure 5.6*) rated at 750 cubic feet per minute cfm can ventilate a 200-barrel tank safely in less than an hour; such blowers are available from most industrial supply sources. The atmosphere should be tested by gas monitor to verify that the hazardous condition has been mitigated.

c. Hazard survey.   Before entering a confined space, the worker should conduct a survey to identify potential hazards, noting pumps and lines that feed into the vessel, steam controls, and drives or controls for mechanical systems, such as mixers or rakes. A lockout-tagout protocol should be followed.

d. Permits.   Approval to enter a confined space should come in the form of a confined space permit. The permit verifies completion of the hazard survey described above. It lists the nature of the work to be performed and specifies entry and exit times. It is the responsibility of the trained worker entering the confined space to perform the necessary checks and to procure the permit. The worker's supervisor signs this permit. Vessels that do not pose an atmospheric hazard, such as ventilated brewhouse tanks and water tanks, may be classified as non-permit-entry tanks, provided that all mechanical hazards are properly locked out and tagged.

Figure 5.6. Portable blower and ducting for tank ventilation. (Courtesy of BridgePort Brewing Company)

e. Attendants.   No worker should enter a permit-required confined space without an attendant present. It is the responsibility of the attendant to stand by and monitor the safety of the person working in the confined space. Communication between the two must be maintained at all times. The attendant must be trained and ready to provide assistance in the event of an emergency. If a rescue becomes necessary, the attendant should never enter the tank but should call 911 for emergency assistance instead. There are many well-documented cases in which would-be but ill-equipped rescuers have perished trying to assist a downed co-worker.

f. Rescue.   A rescue protocol should be established. Brewery management should not wait for the real thing before determining how to respond to a confined space incident. The local fire department or rescue service should be contacted to ascertain whether they are equipped and trained to handle such an emergency. If they are not, other options, such as training and equipping brewery personnel, should be considered.

g. Safety equipment.   Equipment necessary for the job should be purchased. Portable blowers are inexpensive and ventilate tanks quickly and efficiently. A gas monitor is an important verification tool. If vessels must be entered through a top manway, a harness to suspend a person in the upright position and a hoist must be available. Purchase of a self-contained breathing apparatus should also be considered.

17. What personal protection equipment is needed in the brewery?

The following are some basic types of personal protection equipment that should be supplied to workers:

a. Safety glasses, goggles, or face shields are useful when liquids such as caustics and acids are handled. Eye injuries make up the vast majority of safety-related injuries. Eye protection can be ineffective or, even worse, a hazard itself if it is not properly designed, constructed, and fitted. According to OSHA regulations, all devices for eye and face protection should comply with American National Standards Institute (ANSI) standard Z87.1-1989 and should be marked as such by the manufacturer.

b. Gloves are critical for workers handling chemicals and hot fittings. To adequately protect the user from harmful exposure, gloves must be constructed of chemical-resistant rubber, neoprene, or latex. They should be worn with the cuff turned up to prevent chemical solutions from running down the arms in working overhead.

c. Respiratory protection is important in an inadequately ventilated space or when materials such as malt, filter aids such as diatomaceous earth, or even filter pads are handled. Respirators and dust masks offer protection against various hazards, but their effectiveness depends on the construction of the filtering mechanism and media. It is important to use the correct type of respirator for an identified hazard. When a respirator is worn, the wearer must take special measures to ensure that it fits correctly. Respirators and masks must be stored in dust-tight containers to prevent contamination of their filters.

d. Footwear should be required to meet the needs for each area of use. Normally, rubber boots are used in the brewhouse, cellars, and racking room, where water, chemical solutions, and hot wort are hazards. Leather boots may be used in the packaging and warehouse areas, where liquids are not a hazard. Steel-toed footwear and even steel metatarsal protection are highly recommended to protect from injury. All footwear should conform to the appropriate ANSI standards. Open-toed footwear should never be allowed in production areas.

e. Hearing protection equipment includes disposable soft earplugs, custom-molded earplugs, and earmuffs. Proper training in how to insert earplugs is necessary to achieve maximum protection.

18. What can be done to minimize environmental hazards in the brewery?

As previously discussed, environmental hazards in the brewhouse range from elevated noise levels to hazardous atmospheres in confined spaces. Here are a few things to remember:

a. Hearing protection.   Proper hearing protection should be available for all employees. By current OSHA standards, a sound level in the workplace exceeding an 8-hour time-weighted average of 85 decibels (dBA) necessitates the implementation of a hearing conservation program that includes annual hearing tests. Noise levels over 90 dBA during an 8-hour shift of a 40-hour work week exceed the limits established by OSHA.

b. Respiratory protection.   Particulates such as malt dust and diatomaceous earth, both common in the brewery environment, can be hazardous to the respiratory system. It is important to protect employees by providing appropriate ventilators, respirators, dust masks, and filters. If respirators are needed to protect employee health, or if they are required by the employer, OSHA requires that the employer establish and implement a respiratory-protection plan that includes medical evaluation of employees required to use respirators (OSHA reg, 1910.134c).

c. Head protection.   In any area where there is a potential for head injury caused by falling objects, it is important to provide appropriate head protection. Like all personal protective equipment, helmets and hard hats must be constructed according to OSHA standards and must fit the user correctly.

d. Slips and falls.   The brewhouse can be a wet and cluttered environment during production. Water is regularly used to hose down equipment and working surfaces, and hoses may be laid out in all directions. Under these conditions, slips and falls can often occur. It is important that workers in the brewhouse wear appropriate footwear, which should provide traction on slippery surfaces and protect the foot from excessive wetness and exposure to chemicals. In addition, footwear with steel toes and tarsal protection should be worn to protect workers from crushing injuries, which can be caused by heavy equipment such as forklifts or pallet jacks. To minimize tripping hazards, there can be no better measure than to keep walkways and work areas as clear of equipment and clutter as possible and to ensure that the entire brewhouse is well illuminated. Ladders and overhead work platforms should have nonskid decking and should be adequately guarded with rails to prevent falls.

Industrial hygiene services are available (for example, from workers' compensation insurance carriers and the consulting branch of OSHA) to help assess the level of noise and atmospheric and environmental hazards in the plant and are excellent resources for determining the types of protection necessary.

19. How can physical injury caused by handling of materials be prevented?

Ergonomic hazards are common in an environment such as a brewhouse. Unlike catastrophic incidents that cause immediate injury, ergonomic injuries develop over a long period of time. Hence, they may be dismissed or neglected by workers, who continue to perform in the same way until the damage is irreversible. Common ergonomic injuries in the brewhouse are back injuries related to lifting or moving material or equipment. Such injuries can occur when workers perform tasks to which they are unaccustomed, use improper posture or position in performing tasks, or attempt to perform tasks that exceed their physical strength. Other common injuries are the result of repetitive tasks, usually involving the wrists or hands. Factors that lead to repetitive stress injury include force of motion, frequency of repetition, position of the hand, and vibration of the hand.

Ergonomic problems can often be eliminated by using well-designed equipment or by engineering solutions, but the best prevention strategies are worker training and education. Whether workers are lifting bags of malt, moving hoses, or securing clamps for hardpipe connections, it is important that they be aware of the potential hazards. They must be able to identify the movements or positions that contribute to injury in their tasks and know the corrective measures that can be taken to prevent them. Cross-training employees to perform different tasks and then rotating them from task to task can be an effective method for minimizing repetitive motion injuries. Workers' compensation insurance providers or OSHA can refer brewery management to appropriate training materials or services.

20. What is an emergency action plan?

An emergency action plan is a written plan provided by an employer that stipulates actions to be taken by both the employer and the employees to ensure employee safety in the event of an emergency. This plan should include the following:

a. Definitions of emergencies requiring partial or full evacuation

b. Emergency escape procedures and route assignments

c. Procedures for employees who remain behind to perform critical functions

d. Procedures to account for all employees after emergency evacuation

e. Identification of emergency rescue and medical aide duties

f. Preferred means of reporting or announcing emergency evacuations (e.g., intercom, alarms, or horns)

g. Names and job titles of persons or departments who can be contacted for further information about the plan

h. Regular training and drills for employees

21. What precautions can be taken to prevent accidents associated with production equipment?

It is important for the workers to understand what hazards are associated with the use of equipment in their area. Misuse often results from a lack of knowledge of or disregard for proper operating procedure. Proper operator training and thorough maintenance are essential. Accidents related to mechanical hazards include pinching or crushing injuries to fingers or hands caused by moving mechanical parts, such as uncovered drive chains or belts; electrical injuries from improperly grounded or faulty wiring; burns from failed or improper hose and pipe connections; and slips and falls. Injuries such as these can be prevented by rigorous adherence to some basic rules of safety.

a. Electrical shock. All electrical equipment must be properly grounded and securely connected. This is important under the wet conditions common in the brewhouse. Watertight equipment (National Electrical Manufacturers Association [NEMA] type 4) and fittings should be used on all electrical installations.

b. Personal effects. Workers' hair should be tied back or worn under a cap, and any loose clothing should be secured. Workers should remove jewelry, such as chains and bracelets, when working around machines. Footwear must provide adequate traction on wet floors.

c. Machine guards. All guards must be kept in place. Drive belts, chains, and pulleys should be properly covered to prevent injury to operators. Machine door guards should never be deactivated for any reason other than maintenance or inspection. They are specifically intended for the safety of the operator.

d. Moving machinery. Workers should never reach into an operating mill to remove a sample unless the mill has been designed to safely accommodate such action. Triers, which allow for sampling safely from outside the mill, should be installed.

e. Conveyors. Workers should never stand or walk on conveyors. Ladders or platforms should be installed to facilitate access to equipment. Platforms should have adequate railings, proper kickplates, and nonskid surfaces to prevent falls.

f. Regulating equipment. All pressure and temperature gauges should function properly and accurately, and all pressure relief devices should be checked regularly for proper operation.

g. Hose and hardpipe connections. All hose and hardpipe connections should always be double-checked before product is transferred. A switch to a pump should never be activated or a valve opened until the worker has verified that all connections are secure, properly configured, and free of any obstruction. A worker should never stand in front of a valve while opening or activating it.

22. What are some other general safety policies?

a. Dress code. Uniform or clothing requirements should be established and enforced. Clearly, some modes of dress are more conducive to safety in the workplace than others. Loose-fitting clothing and jewelry may be caught in moving machinery.

b. Drug and alcohol use. Company policy must clearly forbid the use of alcohol or drugs during work shifts.

c. Incident or accident documentation. Documentation is an important process and an appropriate function for a safety committee. All workplace accidents must be thoroughly investigated to determine their causes so that preventive or corrective measures can be taken.

d. First aid and emergency care. First-aid stations must be readily accessible to all employees and must be maintained as needed to ensure an adequate supply of materials. Basic first-aid procedures and cardiopulmonary resuscitation (CPR) should be part of employee training. Employees should know how to get to a telephone to call 911 for emergency aid.

e. Fire protection. Fire extinguishers and other fire suppression devices must be readily accessible to all employees. All employees must be familiar with the location and use of these devices.

f. Forklift and vehicle safety.   OSHA requires that a training program be provided for all employees who operate forklifts, and each operator must carry a certification card that can be shown to an inspector. Workers who operate brewery vehicles as part of their jobs should receive ongoing training as part of the company's safety program.

Index